D0476709

A Blueprint for Revival

A Blueprint for Revival
A NEW BIOGRAPHY

Lessons from the Life of John Wesley

Mark Williamson

Authentic

Copyright © 2011 Mark Williamson

17 16 15 14 13 12 11   7 6 5 4 3 2 1

This edition first published 2011 by Authentic Media Limited
Presley Way, Crownhill, Milton Keynes, MK8 0ES
www.authenticmedia.co.uk

The right of Mark Williamson to be identified as the Author of
this Work has been asserted by him in accordance with the
Copyright, Designs and Patents Act 1988

All rights reserved. No part of this publication may be repro-
duced, stored in a retrieval system, or transmitted in any form
or by any means, electronic, mechanical, photocopying,
recording or otherwise, without the prior permission of the
publisher or a licence permitting restricted copying. In the UK
such licences are issued by the Copyright Licensing Agency,
Saffron House, 6–10 Kirby Street, London, EC1N 8TS.

British Library Cataloguing in Publication Data

A catalogue record for this book is available from the
British Library

ISBN 978-1-85078-962-8

Cover design by Huw Tyler Share Creative
Printed and bound in the UK by
CPI Group (UK) Ltd, Croydon, CRO 4YY

Dedicated to Rob Frost, 'one of the greatest
helpers that Mr Wesley ever had'

With thanks to Barrie Tabraham for the generous loan of books, and my wife Joanna for the ideas and encouragement

Contents

Preface – One Rock International

This book is part of a series that has been developed by One Rock International; each book is a biography of a different missionary leader. One Rock International is passionate about empowering Christian leaders to find and fulfil God's vision for their lives, and so further his kingdom in places and ministry contexts all over the globe.

Throughout the history of Christianity, there have been countless examples of missionary leaders who allowed God to do incredible things through them. However, many of their stories and lives are unknown to this generation. These books aim to remind us of all that God has done through individuals in the past, and so give us a greater expectation of what he might do through us in the present and future.

Each book tells the life story of an individual, using many of their own words so we can hear their unique voice. Each aims to be packed with information, brief in length, and readable in style.

At the end of each chapter there are learning summaries, with key points so that leaders in the twenty-first century can learn from these people of history. They are grouped into the four curriculum areas that One Rock resources people in: Spiritual Formation, Discerning

Vision, Leadership Skills and Mission Skills. Each of these is denoted by the following icons:

 Spiritual Formation

 Discerning Vision

 Leadership Skills

 Mission Skills

We hope these books challenge, inspire and inform your leadership for Jesus. For more information and resources, visit www.onerockinternational.com

Foreword

I was excited to hear that Mark Williamson was writing a book about John Wesley, focusing on his leadership strategies, and how these can impact leaders and churches today. I feel honoured to have a chance to both commend the book and make some comments on the material.

This book challenges Christians to reflect and learn from a significant part of the Christian story, and from a figure within our heritage. Mark draws on the life of one of the great men of history to encourage and equip future generations. It is very important for the leaders of today to see that God has been inspiring and using people to shape the church throughout the ages. We should not only look forward to the 'new thing' God has in store, but have a clear understanding of all that has gone before.

Within these pages are tried and tested truths gleaned from the life of one of this country's most outstanding leaders – John Wesley. He was a man whose passion, commitment and strategy changed the face of a nation. The life and works of Wesley have also had an incredible impact on our contemporary church – many of the strategies that Wesley initiated are still used today by numerous churches of varied streams. This book not only identifies these strategies, but also captures the key themes of Wesley's life that are particularly pertinent for the development of strong leaders.

Although this is a slim work, the depth of reflection and insight is extremely significant. If read and absorbed, this book could play a major part in developing leaders and providing the church with strong direction. This resource would be a helpful addition to any reading list on courses which seek to identify and train people in the Church.

This book makes a significant contribution to the growing number of leadership resources. It not only challenges, encourages and equips the reader, but also reminds us of the example Wesley sets for a new and emerging church, and particularly for its leaders.

I commend this book to you.

Ashley Cooper

Reverend Ashley Cooper is Senior Pastor of Swan Bank Church in Stoke-on-Trent, one of the largest Methodist churches in the UK. He is also one of the leaders of the ECG Annual Conference, www.ecgevent.org.uk

1

Childhood

1703–20

In 1703, in Epworth, Lincolnshire, John Wesley was born as the fifteenth of the nineteen children of Reverend Samuel and Susanna Wesley. Both parents would have a lasting influence on their son, who would go on to dramatically shake the nations of England, Ireland, Scotland, Wales and America.

Family Background

There were ten surviving children from the nineteen born to the Wesley family. John's brother Samuel and sisters Emilia, Susanna (whom the family called Sukey), Mary (sometimes Molly), Mehatabel (also called Hetty) and Anne (sometimes Nancy) were all older than him. Born after John were Martha (sometimes Patty), Charles and Kezia.

The Wesleys were a devout Christian family. Both of Wesley's grandfathers were Dissenting ministers – Christian ministers who had chosen to leave the Church of England, either to become independent or to join other denominations. Therefore, both Samuel and Susanna grew up as Dissenters, but chose to join the Anglican Church as young adults. This common religious background and journey was one similarity that attracted them to each other.

However, Samuel and Susanna did not always agree, and a temporary separation between them in early 1702 nearly ensured John was never even born. In politics, Samuel was a supporter of King William III, a Protestant Dutch prince installed as King of England, Ireland and Scotland by the English parliament in 1689 to ensure England remained a Protestant nation. Susanna preferred James II, the deposed king who had the legitimate title, but who was also Roman Catholic. Each night Samuel Wesley would pray for the health of the king. Susanna would acknowledge the prayer, but would take 'king' to refer to the exiled King James, not the ruling King William. When James II died, she stopped joining in the prayer, and because of this difference of opinion her husband claimed their marriage was over, made a foolish vow, and irresponsibly left her.

An Abandoned Wife

You advise me to continue with my husband, and God knows how gladly I would do it, but there, there is my supreme affliction, he will not live with me. 'Tis but a little while since he one evening observed in our family prayers that I did not say Amen to his prayer for King William as I usually do to all others; upon which he retired to his study, and calling me to him asked the reason of my not saying Amen to the prayer. I was a little surprised at the question and don't know well what I answered, but too well I remember what followed; he immediately kneeled down and imprecated the divine vengeance upon himself and all his posterity if ever he touched me more or came into a bed with me before I had begged God's pardon and his for not saying Amen to the prayer for the king.

This, madam, is my unhappy case. I've unsuccessfully represented to him the unlawfulness and unreasonableness of his oath . . . that since I'm willing to let him quietly enjoy his opinions, he ought not to deprive me of my little liberty of conscience. But he has opened his mouth to the Lord . . . I have no resentment against my master, so far from it that the very next day I went with him to the communion, though he that night forsook my bed, to which he has been a stranger ever since.

Letter from Susanna Wesley to Lady Yarborough,
7 March 1702

Samuel made his vow on 1 March 1702, and left the family home on 5 April 1702. He went to London, and began negotiating with the navy to become a ship's chaplain, and consequently travel overseas. It was only two events that brought him home – King William III had died on 8 March 1702 and was succeeded by Queen Anne, but more importantly the Wesley family home was partially destroyed by fire on 31 July 1702.

With Queen Anne becoming the unchallenged monarch, the reason for the dispute was removed, and the house fire was interpreted by Samuel as a sign from God that his vow had in some way been fulfilled, and that he should return home. He rejoined his family and his wife in August 1702 after an absence of four months. John Wesley was born some ten months later, in June 1703, a fruit – and a permanent sign – of their reconciliation. He would go on to inherit the deep religious convictions and scholarly intellects of both his parents. But he would follow more in the footsteps of his logical and reasoning mother, rather than his impulsive father.

Samuel Wesley

Reverend Samuel Wesley was a vicar, an amateur poet, a staff writer for a religious newspaper and an aspiring theologian. He was unpopular as a church leader – services at Epworth were poorly attended, and many of the parishioners felt he was too harsh in his judgements upon them. He was also a poor manager of his family finances. To help bring more money in, Samuel tried his hand at farming, but his crops were burned and his milk cows were maimed, quite possibly by opponents who disliked him. Rather than making money, such ventures drove him further into debt, a condition he was in throughout his adult life.

His unpopularity and his debt both came to a head in 1705. During an election campaign, Samuel began by enthusiastically backing one candidate, but then publicly switched sides halfway through. This enraged his former colleagues, one of whom had lent him £30. This man called in the debt, but Samuel could not pay, and was arrested and sent to Lincoln prison until the money was paid off. During his several months in prison, he wrote to friends and colleagues for financial help.

Although sometimes an impulsive and reckless character, the positive side to his emotionalism was a burning passion for God, and for mission. Whilst in prison his letters to the Archbishop of York show this side of Samuel's character – he was someone always looking for opportunities to share the gospel.

Prison Letters

[25 June 1705] I don't despair of doing some good here . . . and it may be I shall do more in this new parish than in my old; for I have leave to read prayers every morning and afternoon here in the prison, and to preach once a Sunday . . . And I'm getting acquainted with my brother jail-birds as fast as I can; and shall write to London to the Society for Propagating Christian Knowledge, who, I hope, will send me some books to distribute among them.

[12 September 1705] Most of my friends advise me to leave Epworth, if e'er I should get from hence. I confess I am not of that mind, because I may yet do good there; and 'tis like a coward to desert my post because the enemy fire thick upon me. They have only wounded me yet, and, I believe, can't kill me. I hope to be at home by Xmas. God help my poor family!

Letters from Samuel Wesley to
Archbishop of York[2]

Samuel Wesley had a profound impact on his son John. He had an enthusiasm for mission work, whether in debtors' prisons, or through a proposed scheme for sending missionaries to India. He was a Christian scholar and an intellectual of his day – his chief literary work was a colossal Latin commentary on the book of Job. John Wesley learned about zeal for the Lord and rigorous scholarship from his father, but he also learned of the need for discipline to be mixed with grace, and the importance of managing personal finances properly.

A Rectory Fire

On 9 February 1709 the Wesley house was burned down again, and like before there were rumours of angry parishioners possibly being responsible. By now John was 6 years old and he barely escaped this fire with his life. Susanna related the incident to her eldest son Samuel who was away at boarding school in Westminster:

A Miraculous Escape

We had no time to take our clothes . . . I called to Betty to bring the children out of the nursery; she took up Patty, and left Jacky [John] to follow her, but he going to the door and seeing all on fire, ran back again. . . .

When I was in the yard I looked about for your father and the children; but, seeing none, concluded them all lost.

But, thank God, I was mistaken! Your father carried sister Emily, Suky, and Patty into the garden; then, missing Jacky, he ran back into the house, to see if he could save him. He heard him miserably crying out in the nursery, and attempted several times to get upstairs, but was beat back by the flames; then he thought him lost, and commended his soul to God, and went to look after the rest. The child climbed up to the window, and called out to them in the yard; they got up to the casement, and pulled him out just as the roof fell into the chamber. Harry broke the glass in the parlour window, and threw out your sisters Mary and Hetty; and so, by God's great mercy, we all escaped.

Letter from Susanna Wesley to Samuel Wesley Jnr,
14 February 1709

John Wesley's own account of his rescue was written down nearly seventy years later, towards the end of his life. It shows how close he would have come to death had it not been for the resourcefulness and bravery of two of his neighbours. Both Susanna, and later John Wesley himself, came to refer to this incident as a sign of divine purpose over his life – that he had been spared for a reason. Susanna would later talk about her son as 'a brand plucked from the burning', a reference to verses from Amos 4:11 and Zechariah 3:2, and a quote that Wesley would go on to use many times in reference to himself.

A Brand Plucked from the Burning

I remember all the circumstances as distinctly as though it were but yesterday. Seeing the room was very light, I called to the maid to take me up. But none answering, I put my head out of the curtains and saw streaks of fire on the top of the room. I got up and ran to the door, but could get no farther, all the door beyond it being in a blaze. I then climbed up on the chest, which stood near the window; one in the yard saw me, and proposed running to fetch a ladder. Another answered, 'There will not be time; but I have thought of another expedient. Here I will fix myself against the wall; lift a light man, and set him upon my shoulders.' They did so, and he took me out of the window. Just then the whole roof fell in; but it fell inward, or we had all been crushed at once. When they brought me into the house where my father was, he cried out, 'Come, neighbours, let us kneel down; let us give thanks to God! He has given me all my eight children; let the house go; I am rich enough.' The next day, as he was walking in the garden and surveying the ruins of the house, he picked up part of a leaf of his Polyglot Bible, on which just those words were legible: 'Go; sell all that thou hast; and take up thy cross, and follow me.'

Wesley, The Arminian Magazine,
January 1778[4]

Susanna Wesley

Susanna was the biggest influence on the young Wesley as he grew up. She took on the responsibility of educating all her children, ensuring they grew spiritually and morally, as well as intellectually. She succeeded so well that all three of her sons became clergymen and university graduates, while her daughters were educated far beyond most other young women in England. A letter to her husband shows the time and dedication she devoted to each child:

I take such a proportion of time as I can best spare every night to discourse with each child by itself, on something that relates to its principal concerns. On Monday I talk with Molly, on Tuesday with Hetty, Wednesday with Nancy, Thursday with Jacky, Friday with Patty, Saturday with Charles; and with Emily and Sukey together on Sunday.

Letter from Susanna Wesley to Samuel Wesley,
6 February 1712[5]

From his mother's schoolroom, Wesley learned the values of routine, rhythm, discipline, the need for spiritual and intellectual growth, and the importance of surrendering his will to another. This act of surrender was a foundational point in Susanna's method, and the place she began when educating any child.

Susanna Wesley's Home School Methods

When turned a year old (and some before), they were taught to fear the rod, and to cry softly; by which means they escaped abundance of correction they might otherwise have had, and that most odious noise of the crying of children was rarely heard in the house. . . .

In order to form the minds of children, the first thing to be done is to conquer their will, and bring them to an obedient temper. . . . For, by neglecting timely correction, they will contract a stubbornness and obstinacy which is hardly ever after conquered; and never, without using such severity as would be painful to me as to the child. In the esteem of the world they pass for kind and indulgent whom I call cruel parents, who permit their children to get habits which they know must be afterwards broken. . . .

The children of this family were taught, as soon as they could speak, the Lord's Prayer, which they were made to say at rising and bed-time constantly; to which, as they grew bigger, were added a short prayer for their parents, and some collects; a short catechism, and some portions of Scripture, as their memories could bear. . . .

They were quickly made to understand they might have nothing they cried for, and instructed to speak handsomely for what they wanted. . . .

There was no such thing as loud talking or playing allowed of, but every one was kept close to their business, for the six hours of school: and it is almost incredible what a child may be taught in a quarter of a year, by a vigorous application, if it have but a tolerable capacity and good health. . . .

There were several by-laws observed among us . . .

1. It had been observed that cowardice and fear of punishment often led children into lying, till they get a custom of it, which they cannot leave. To prevent this a law was made, that whoever was charged with a fault, of which they were guilty, if they would ingenuously confess it, and promise to amend, should not be beaten. This rule prevented a great deal of lying . . .
2. That no sinful action, as lying, pilfering, playing at church, or on the Lord's day, disobedience, quarrelling, etc, should ever pass unpunished.

3. That no child should ever be chid or beat twice for the same fault; and that, if they amended, they should never be upbraided with it afterwards.
4. That every signal act of obedience, especially when it crossed upon their own inclinations, should always be commended, and frequently rewarded, according to the merits of the cause.
5. That if ever any child performed an act of obedience, or did anything with an intention to please, though the performance was not well, yet the obedience and intention should be kindly accepted; and the child with sweetness directed how to do better for the future.
6. That propriety be inviolably preserved, and none suffered to invade the property of another in the smallest matter, though it were but of the value of a farthing or a pin . . .
7. That promises be strictly observed; and a gift once bestowed, and so the right passed away from the donor, be not resumed, but left to the disposal of him to whom it was given . . .
8. That no girl be taught to work till she can read very well.

Letter from Susanna Wesley to John Wesley,
24 July 1732[6]

Susanna was a devout Christian, and an intensely strong-willed woman. Both these qualities came to the fore during the winter of 1711–12. Her husband was away in London on a prolonged visit, so Susanna began reading stories of Danish missionaries to her children and servants in order to provide some family devotions. Others heard about what she was doing and started to assemble in the house on a Sunday afternoon, so that they could hear the readings and join the Wesley family in prayers. These house meetings grew from twenty to forty, until eventually around two hundred people were crammed into the Wesley family kitchen, hungry to hear stories of God. The numbers were far larger than those who came to the Epworth Sunday morning services, and this aroused the jealousy of the local curate who was preaching in place of Samuel Wesley. He complained to Samuel, who in turn wrote from London asking his wife to stop the meetings. If it had become known, a female layperson conducting religious meetings would have caused a scandal in the Church of England, but Susanna's reply to her husband displays both the passion and the determination she could show in the cause of Christ:

> If you do, after all, think fit to dissolve this assembly, do not tell me that you desire me to do it, for that will not satisfy my conscience; but send me your positive command, in such full and express terms as may absolve me from all guilt and punishment, for neglecting this opportunity of doing good, when you and I shall appear before the great and awful tribunal of our Lord Jesus Christ.
>
> *Letter from Susanna Wesley to Samuel Wesley,*
> *24 February 1712*[7]

Needless to say, Samuel left this letter unanswered, and the house meetings continued. They had a profound impact on the young Wesley, who would take from his mother not only a sound education but also the belief that it was lawful to disagree with, and take on, the established church authorities if the result was seeing more people drawn to religious meetings, and therefore drawn into a relationship with God.

In 1714 at the age of 10, John Wesley left home for Charterhouse in London – a boarding school where he would live for the next seven years, and where his knowledge of Greek, Latin, philosophy and algebra would be brought up to a standard ready for university. He reported that he was sometimes bullied, and had his dinner stolen by the older boys so frequently that he later claimed he mainly survived on bread and water. Despite the learning he received at Charterhouse, the education and experiences he had there paled in comparison to the effect that his parents, a house fire and some inspired meetings would have on his character.

Childhood

Key learning points

Spiritual Formation

Education is crucial. One of the greatest aims of a good education should be to create a hunger for continual spiritual and intellectual growth. The education Wesley's mother gave him started a life-long passion for learning, and gave him a basis for achievement.

Balance passion with reason. Both passion and reason are important, but the most productive lives are not swayed solely by one or the other; they maintain a healthy and powerful balance of both.

Avoid debt. Debt can ruin an individual and a family, and even lead to imprisonment. The example of his father taught Wesley the importance of financial stewardship, and of always living within his level of income.

Cultivate honesty. Learning to be honest from an early age makes integrity all the more likely in adulthood.

Discerning Vision

Parents influence us. The greatest influence on the young Wesley was his parents. He inherited their many good characteristics, but chose not to repeat their mistakes.

Experiences shape us. The powerful childhood experience of being rescued from a fire shaped Wesley's view of his life and calling.

Mission Skills

Prioritize mission. Saving souls is more important than conforming to church traditions. Using methods that push the boundaries of convention in order to reach people should always be welcomed, provided they are biblical.

2

The Religious Zealot

1720–35

Wesley entered Christchurch College at Oxford University in 1720. The city would be his main home for the next fifteen years, and see the beginnings of a movement that would go on to impact the whole world for Christ.

Vocational Decisions

Wesley mainly studied classics and logic at university. He was not especially religious or devout during this period of his life. He only attended church services three times a year, and although he still recited daily the prayers he had learned in childhood, his heart was not in them. He was more concerned with literature and philosophy – and with swimming and card playing – than with thoughts of God.

This continued until late 1724 when, as a 21-year-old man, he began to think seriously about what career he should pursue upon leaving university. With his father, both his grandfathers, and now his older brother Samuel all being clergymen, the most natural and most expected decision was for him to follow in their footsteps. His mother had already written to him, encouraging him to become ordained, so he could return home to Epworth and help his father. Wesley preferred the idea of remaining in Oxford and becoming a lecturer, but doing this also required him to become ordained. Since the two careers both had the same requirements, he wrote to his parents explaining that he was considering ordination. He also asked for their advice because he was unsure that he was living a sufficiently holy life for such a call.

His father suggested he delay, and spend a year or so studying the Scriptures in their original languages of Hebrew, Aramaic and Greek – whilst also learning Syrian – to gain a better biblical understanding: 'You ask me which is the best commentary on the Bible. I answer, the Bible' (letter from Samuel Wesley to John Wesley, 26 January 1725).[1] His mother's answer was more pastoral:

The Beginnings of a Devotional Life

I heartily wish you would now enter upon a serious examination of yourself, that you may know whether you have a reasonable hope of salvation; that is, whether you are in a state of faith and repentance or not, which you know are the conditions of the gospel covenant on our part. . . . Now I mention this, it calls to mind your letter to your father about taking orders. I was much pleased with it, and liked the proposal well; but it is an unhappiness almost peculiar to our family, that your father and I seldom think alike.

Letter from Susanna Wesley to John Wesley,
23 February 1725

His mother believed that studying theology in preparation for ordination would draw Wesley closer to God, and by March 1725 she had persuaded her husband to agree with her. In that same month Wesley followed his mother's advice on self-examination, and began keeping a diary to record in detail the temptations and sins that he faced.

Spiritual Growth

During the spring of 1725, Wesley also made new friends and read new books that would contribute to his spiritual growth. He became close friends with a fellow Oxford resident named Robin Griffiths. Robin's father, who was a vicar in Gloucestershire, introduced them to a local clergyman, Reverend Lionel Kirkham, who had a son and three daughters all near in age to Wesley and Robin. Wesley would go on to become a little infatuated with Sally Kirkham, and to a lesser extent with her younger sister, Betty. These sisters encouraged him to read *The Christian Pattern*, an English translation of the medieval devotional classic, *The Imitation of Christ* by Thomas à Kempis. Around the same time he also read *Holy Living and Dying* by Jeremy Taylor.

Through the influence of these books, and the company of the Kirkham family, Wesley saw that if he were to be ordained he should give his whole life and heart to serving God. He began studying theology in preparation for his ordination, and set out on a regime of weekly attendance at communion and intense self-examination. He also started to formulate for himself and Robin Griffiths a set of religious rules to live their lives by, many being taken from Jeremy Taylor's book. At this time the great Christian truth of justification by faith had been forgotten by much of the Church of England, and Wesley was not alone in believing that he must earn his salvation through striving for good works, and living a pure and holy life. His diary entries and his resolve therefore centred on the sins he discovered through his journey of self-examination, and on human rules for overcoming them.

First Diary Entry

I found a great many unclean thoughts arise in prayer, and discovered these temptations to it:

  a. Too much addicting myself to a light behaviour at all times;
  b. Listening too much to idle talk, and reading vain plays and books;
  c. Idleness; and lastly
  d. Want of due consideration in whose presence I am.

From which I perceive it is necessary

  a. To labour for a grave and modest carriage;
  b. To avoid vain and light company; and
  c. To entertain awful apprehensions of the presence of God;
  d. To avoid idleness, freedom with women, and high seasoned meats;
  e. To resist the very beginnings of lust, not by arguing with, but by thinking no more of it or by immediately going into company; lastly
  f. To use frequent and fervent prayer.

General Rules as to Intention

1. In every action reflect on your end;
2. Begin every action in the name of the Father, the Son, and the Holy Ghost;
3. Begin every important work with prayer;
4. Do not leave off a duty because you are tempted in it.

Wesley's Diary, 26 March 1725

Reverend John Wesley

Wesley was ordained as a deacon within the Church of England on 19 September 1725. He had no church of his own, but would fill in for clergymen away on business by taking Sunday services at parishes in Oxfordshire and Buckinghamshire. His real desire was still to lecture at Oxford, rather than settle down in a parish, and in March 1726 he received a great boost to this career plan by being elected a Fellow of Lincoln College at Oxford University. To begin with he would only have very light teaching duties, but an academic life now opened up before him.

Sally Kirkham had married a local schoolteacher in December 1725, but Wesley still remained close friends with both her and Betty Kirkham, writing regularly, and spending Christmases with the Kirkham family. The spiritual nature of their conversations continued to deepen Wesley's desire for salvation and holiness, and the death of Robin Griffiths in January 1727 from tuberculosis made him all the more concerned with ensuring – as his mother had written to him – that he had 'a reasonable hope of salvation'. He continued with his routine of rules and self-examination, but the death of Robin took away from him the one friend who had been trying to join him in living such a strict way of life. His younger brother, Charles, had now moved to Oxford to begin studying at the university, and Wesley repeatedly invited Charles to become a fellow Christian friend on the journey to holiness. However, Charles was more interested in enjoying the freedom of being a student, and would reply to his brother, 'What! would you have me become a saint all at once?' (letter from Charles Wesley to Dr Thomas Chandler, 28 April 1785).[3]

Wesley's teaching duties as a Fellow at Lincoln College were so light that he spent most of the two years from August 1727 to August 1729 back at home in Epworth, assisting as a curate in a new church his father had taken on at the nearby village of Wroote. During this time, he was further ordained as a priest on 22 September 1728. But it was only at the request of his parents that he spent so long away from Oxford, and he was relieved when his college recalled him in autumn 1729 to lecture in logic, Greek and philosophy.

The Holy Club

Whilst Wesley was at home in Epworth, in Oxford Charles had undergone a change of heart towards religion. An infatuation with an actress had come and gone. This left him with an acute realization of his own fallen nature, and a desire to seek salvation. In January 1729 Charles began to keep a daily diary, using the same method of examination and introspection as his brother. He also gathered together two friends, and encouraged them to join him in taking communion at the cathedral worship each week, much as Wesley had begun doing four years previously. One of these was Robert Kirkham, younger brother of Sally and Betty. The other was a young man named William Morgan.

Charles had persuaded these friends to join him at weekly worship, but he knew that for the three of them to grow in holiness they needed the advice of someone who had already walked further down the path. He wrote to his brother, asking him to come back to Oxford and lead the three of them towards spiritual perfection. Wesley had the opportunity when he moved back to Oxford in November 1729. On his return, he immediately became the leader of this little group of pilgrims, and established a strict regime, comprising of church attendance, Scripture reading and self-examination – he believed that all these disciplines were necessary for saving a person's soul. The group became notorious amongst the university students, and they were derisively nicknamed the Holy Club, or the Godly Club.

The Beginnings of the Holy Club

In November 1729, at which time I came to reside at Oxford, your son [Morgan], my brother, myself, and one more [Kirkham] agreed to spend three or four evenings in a week together. Our design was to read over the classics, which we had before read in private, on common nights, and on Sunday some book in divinity. In the summer following, Mr Morgan told me he had called at the jail, to see a man who was condemned for killing his wife; and that, from the talk he had with one of the debtors, he verily believed it would do much good if any one would be at the pains of now and then speaking with them. This he so frequently repeated, that on the 24th of August, 1730, my brother and I walked with him to the Castle. We were so well satisfied with our conversation there, that we agreed to go thither once or twice a week; which we had not done long, before he desired me to go with him to see a poor woman in the town who was sick. In this employment too, when we came to reflect upon it, we believed it would be worth while to spend an hour or two in a week; provided the minister of the parish in which any such person was were not against it. . . .

Soon after, a gentleman of Merton College, who was one of our little company, which now consisted of five persons, acquainted us that he had been much rallied the day before for being a member of the Holy Club; and that it was become a common topic of mirth at his college. . . .

We still continued to meet together as usual, and to confirm one another, as well as we could, in our resolutions, to communicate [take holy communion] as often as we had opportunity (which is here once a week); and do what service we could to our acquaintance, the prisoners, and two or three poor families in the town.

Letter from John Wesley to Richard Morgan,
18 October 1732[4]

The Holy Club began as a group of introspective friends, seeking to find salvation through the established spiritual disciplines of Scripture reading, taking communion, and becoming accountable to one another as a group. They initially had no concern for the needs of the outside

world, and it was only William Morgan's persistent challenge to Wesley that led the group to begin serving the
needs of others. They started visiting the prisons and the
sick to bring spiritual comfort. By 1731 their good works
had grown to also include raising money to help those in
need, buying medicine for the sick, and financially help-
ing the debtors in prison. In spring 1731 they began a
small school for poor children in Oxford, and raised the
necessary money to pay a teacher's salary.

The Holy Club never had a large membership, and it
was never an official society or organization. Rather, it
was a group of friends who gathered around Wesley
because they wanted to grow in personal holiness, and
because they recognized him as a leader in this area.
Through his example, they trained themselves to become
ever more strict and methodical in their means of finding
holiness, but they also became involved in local mission
work around Oxford. The group were mainly comprised
of zealous students who had Wesley as a tutor. Most
members would stay in Oxford for the three or four years
of their degree, and would then move on to become clergymen around the country. Notable members, apart from
John and Charles Wesley, included John Gambold (who
later became a bishop of the Moravian Church), James
Hervey (later a theologian and religious writer) and
George Whitefield, who worked with the Wesley brothers, and was a powerful preaching evangelist in both
Britain and America.

Methodical Spiritual Discipline

As the leader of this group, Wesley now became ever
more serious about his search for spiritual perfection. He

became more conscientious in his use of time, seeking to do nothing which was not contributing either to his own or someone else's spiritual growth. He began walking everywhere to save money – even walking from Oxford to Epworth when visiting his parents during the holidays. He discovered he could still read books as he walked, thus maximizing his time whilst travelling. He stopped lighting a fire in his room unless he had guests – again to save expense, and to serve as a form of spiritual penance. He also trained himself to rise at 4 a.m. each morning, to spend an hour in private prayer and devotion before breakfast.

In 1732 a young man named John Clayton joined the Holy Club, and encouraged the group in another spiritual discipline that had been largely forgotten by the church – fasting. Clayton got them to fast on Wednesdays and Fridays. In the same year, Wesley read *A Serious Call to a Devout and Holy Life* by William Law, and came to believe that all human action could be governed by religious laws (either biblical or human), and so he became ever more convinced of the need to create rules and guidelines to cover every eventuality. It was during this time that the Holy Club came to be known as Methodists, due to the strict methodical nature that they applied to every area of life.

Books that Impacted Wesley in Oxford

1725 – *The Christian's Pattern*, a George Stanhope paraphrase of *The Imitation of Christ* by Thomas à Kempis. From this book, Wesley realized the importance of the heart in religious affairs – obeying laws and outward shows of holiness were worthless if the heart was not involved.

1725 – *Holy Living and Dying*, Jeremy Taylor
Having read this book, Wesley began examining his life, and sought to form a series of laws that could govern a holy life. There was therefore sometimes a creative tension between what he learned from Taylor about external rules for holiness, and what he learned from à Kempis about the importance of the heart.

1732 – *A Serious Call to a Devout and Holy Life*, William Law
From this, Wesley saw how comprehensive the law of God both was, and could be. He believed at this time that he was in a state of salvation because he continually sought to keep and obey the law.

Wesley later realized that, during this point of his life, he had been confusing salvation with sanctification. He wanted to ensure his own salvation, but thought he could do this through the strict spiritual schedule he developed for himself and his followers. At this time, he did not realize that salvation was a free gift from God through all that Jesus had done for him. However, the time spent with God through his use of spiritual disciplines contributed towards him eventually finding a deeper understanding of the truth of salvation. After that revelation, which came in 1738, Wesley continued with many of his strict devotional guidelines, but they were all done out of a desire for spending time with God, rather than because of a fear of not attaining salvation. Later quotes from him demonstrate his continuing zeal for spiritual disciplines, but the purpose of them was now completely changed.

Spiritual Disciplines Practised by the Holy Club

Prayer

Wesley trained himself to get up at 4 a.m. each morning to spend the first hour of the day in private prayer. He also began and ended important work with prayer, and at the start of each hour stopped what he was doing for a brief prayer, termed an 'ejaculatory'.

Bible Study

The Scriptures were constantly read and studied in their original translations. The group also studied the writings of the early Church Fathers and other commentaries or interpretations of the Bible.

Holy Communion

Members received communion at Oxford Cathedral once a week, whereas most students would only worship there three times a year. It was because they received the sacrament so regularly that early Methodists were sometimes mistaken for, or labelled as, Roman Catholics.

Journaling

Wesley encouraged members to keep a daily diary, where they would record how they spent each hour of their time and so ensure all their time was spent profitably. In addition to this, once a week (usually on a Saturday evening) Wesley would retreat to his study to review his use of the previous week, and to list the temptations to sin he was facing.

Fasting

From 1732 the group fasted every Wednesday and Friday.

All members of the Holy Club were expected to submit themselves to these disciplines of holiness. By practising them as a community, the group held each other accountable. During the Oxford years, they were practised by Wesley out of a misguided desire to find salvation. After 1738 they continued – although the emphasis on recording the use of *every* hour within journaling was lessened – but they were done out of love rather than fear, and to enable Wesley and the other Methodists different opportunities for meeting with God.

Later Quotes from Wesley on Spiritual Disciplines

On spiritual disciplines: 'The chief of these means are prayer, whether in secret or with the great congregation; searching the Scriptures (which implies reading, hearing and meditating thereon); and receiving the Lord's Supper, eating bread and drinking wine in remembrance of Him'.

Sermon XII, Forty-Four Sermons[5]

On prayer: 'God does nothing but in answer to prayer'.

A Plain Account of Christian Perfection, *1765*[6]

On the Bible: 'I want to know one thing – the way to heaven; how to land safe on that happy shore. God Himself has condescended to teach the way; for this very reason He came from heaven. He hath written it down in a book. O give me that book! At any price, give me the book of God! I have it; here is knowledge enough for me. Let me be a man of one book'.

Preface, Forty-Four Sermons, *1746*[7]

Leaving Oxford

By 1734 Wesley had established much of what he wanted in life. He was an Oxford lecturer with a comfortable salary. He believed he had found the key to spiritual religion through his methodical use of spiritual disciplines. And through the Holy Club, he was having a profound effect on a handful of his students each year, who he believed would then take his rules and his methods with them when they graduated from university. But his life was about to dramatically change.

His father was now 70, and growing close to death. His dying wish was for Wesley to return to Epworth permanently, and take up the work of being vicar to the Epworth flock. This would also allow Wesley's mother, and the remaining family members, to stay living in the Epworth vicarage. But in a series of letters to his parents, and his elder brother Samuel, Wesley flatly refused to leave his academic life in Oxford:

> In the state wherein I am, I can most promote . . . holiness in myself, because I now enjoy several advantages which are almost peculiar to it. . . .
>
> I conclude that where I am most holy myself, there I could most promote holiness in others; and consequently that I could more promote it here than in any place under heaven. . . .
>
> He that took care of the poor sheep before you was born will not forget them when you are dead'.
>
> *Letter from John Wesley to Samuel Wesley,*
> *10 December 1734*[8]

Wesley returned home to Epworth in April 1735, three weeks before his father's death. Under pressure from his whole family, he finally agreed to take over the parish. But it was too late – the church had already been awarded to someone else. He remained in Epworth to hear his father frequently repeat to him, 'The inward witness, son, the inward witness . . . that is the proof, the strongest proof, of Christianity' (letter from John Wesley to John Smith, 22 March 1748).[9] The dying rector also laid his hands on Charles's head and prophesied, 'Be steady! The Christian faith will surely revive in this kingdom. You shall see it, though I shall not' (letter from Charles Wesley to Samuel Wesley Jnr, 30 April 1735).[10] He died shortly afterwards.

A Missionary Overseas

Wesley remained in Epworth for two weeks after his father's death, but he did not return to Oxford as planned. During the last months of his life, Samuel Wesley had again begun talking about various foreign missionary opportunities. His final favourite scheme had been Georgia, a new colony for debtors and religious Dissenters on the eastern seaboard of America. With his background in debt and Dissent, it was natural the dying rector should talk much of it. Wesley had recently met James Oglethorpe, the founder and governor of the colony, when he had preached in Westminster. Oglethorpe wanted pastors for the principal towns of Georgia. He and another Georgia trustee sought to persuade Wesley to join up. Wesley saw the opportunity of preaching Christianity and trying out his Oxford rules on a whole new group of people: the Native American Indians who lived beyond the borders of the colony.

Wesley persuaded his brother Charles and two others, Benjamin Ingham (also an Oxford Methodist) and Charles Delamotte, to join him in sailing for Georgia. Charles was hastily ordained for the mission field, although he was officially going as secretary to Oglethorpe. Wesley was going to take up the role of pastor in the Georgian capital of Savannah, but he and Ingham planned to become missionaries to the Indian tribes after a short stay there. However, in amongst all these motives, the greatest one for Wesley was still his own search for sanctification:

Our end in leaving our native country was not to avoid want, God having given us plenty of temporal blessings, nor to gain riches or honour, which we trust He will ever enable us to look on as no other than dung and dross; but singly this – to save our souls, to live wholly to the glory of God.

Wesley's Journal, 14 October 1735

The Religious Zealot

Key learning points

Spiritual Formation

Accountability is key. Share life's pilgrimage with a Christian friend. A deep spiritual friendship can bring encouragement in hard times, and discipline to withstand temptations.

Journal and reflect. Self-awareness can be one of the most powerful forms of knowledge. Keeping a journal to record his sins, weaknesses and temptations, plus his prayers and any powerful experiences, became a lifelong habit for Wesley.

Practise spiritual disciplines. Spend regular time with God through daily prayer, Bible study and other disciplines (fasting, meditation, worship, etc.). There is no short cut to intimacy with God; spending time with him is the only way.

Discerning Vision

Discuss vocation with the right people. Parents will be a key influence, but Christian friends, mentors, and colleagues can all help in discerning the purpose of your life.

Read the right books. Three key books on spirituality changed Wesley's life, opening up new worlds of ideas and knowledge to him. He continued to be an avid reader all his life.

Mission Skills

Chance encounters are not always chance. Sometimes, one-off meetings with people can lead to profound changes of direction in life. Wesley's meeting with Oglethorpe in Westminster led to him becoming a missionary in America.

3

The Failed Missionary

1735–38

On 14 October 1735 Wesley boarded the ship *Simmonds*, bound for the American colony of Georgia. He left with high hopes of converting the Native American tribes to Christianity. He would return in less than three years, and would consider his mission to have been an utter failure.

Moravian Influence

For their four months on board the ship, the Wesley brothers, Benjamin Ingham and Charles Delamotte created a strict regime similar to the rules of the Oxford Holy Club. They divided the hours of the day into personal devotions, corporate prayer and Bible study, holding worship services for the passengers and crew, and talking with individuals about their state of salvation. To all these activities Wesley now added learning German. On the ship were twenty-six Moravians, missionaries from Germany, also sailing for Georgia. Wesley was impressed with their piety and humility, and later, during a terrifying storm in the Atlantic Ocean, he also became impressed with their bravery in the face of death. He began to realize that these Moravians had a depth of faith and Christian experience that eluded him, despite all of his strict Oxford rules.

Moravian Faith

In the midst of the psalm wherewith their service began, the sea broke over, split the mainsail in pieces, covered the ship, and poured in between the decks, as if the great deep had already swallowed us up. A terrible screaming began among the English. The Germans calmly sung on. I asked one of them afterwards, 'Was you not afraid?' He answered, 'I thank God, no.' I asked, 'But were not your women and children afraid?' He replied mildly, 'No; our women and children are not afraid to die.'

Wesley's Journal, 25 January 1736

He took up German so he could talk with, and learn from, this new religious group. In Georgia he hoped the Germans and the English would be able to work together as missionaries in the New World. Upon arrival, he met with August Spangenberg, one of their leaders, and again realized there was something missing in his own Christian experience.

Searching Questions

I asked Mr Spangenberg's advice with regard to myself – to my own conduct. He told me he could say nothing till he had asked me two or three questions. 'Do you know yourself? Have you the witness within yourself? Does the Spirit of God bear witness with your spirit that you are a child of God?' I was surprised, and knew not what to answer. He observed it, and asked, 'Do you know Jesus Christ?' I paused, and said, 'I know He is the Saviour of the world.' 'True,' replied he; 'but do you know He has saved you?' I answered, 'I hope He has died to save me.' He only added, 'Do you know yourself?' I said, 'I do.' But I fear they were vain words.

Wesley's Journal, 8 February 1736

Unsuccessful Pastors

From the beginning of their arrival, the English missionaries ran into trouble. Wesley and Delamotte stayed in the Georgian capital of Savannah, where Wesley was installed as pastor of the church. Charles Wesley and Ingham left for the town of Frederica, 100 miles to the south, where Charles would act as pastor, as well as being secretary to Governor Oglethorpe. However, Charles's tenure of the parish did not run smoothly. Two married women from his church both confessed to him that they were having affairs with Oglethorpe. They then told Oglethorpe that Charles was spreading gossip about them. Neither of their claims was true, but the mistrust they created between Charles and Oglethorpe was enough for the former to be arrested by the latter. Wesley had to head down to Frederica to negotiate his brother's release. Charles decided after this ordeal, and because of recurrent illness due to the climate, that he would return home. He left for England in July 1736, after just five months in America.

Wesley and Ingham agreed to take over Charles's Frederica church between them. Wesley also took on the role of Oglethorpe's secretary, in addition to his pastoral role in Savannah. He therefore regularly had to make the hazardous journey between the two towns. This lasted several days, and consisted of dangerous boat trips and hiking through marshland.

Wesley was not a popular pastor in either of the towns. His high churchmanship, and the strict requirements he placed on the people to adhere to his own Oxford rules, ensured that he did not gain a ready following.

Wesley's Unpopularity

Observing much coldness in Mr Horton's behaviour, I asked him the reason of it. He answered, 'I like nothing you do. All your sermons are satires upon particular persons, therefore I will never hear you more; and all the people are of my mind, for we won't hear ourselves abused.

'Besides, they say you are Protestants. But as for you, they cannot tell what religion you are of. They never heard of such religion before. They do not know what to make of it. And then your private behaviour – all the quarrels that have been here since you came have been 'long of you. Indeed, there is neither man nor woman in the town who minds a word you say. And so you may preach long enough; but nobody will come to hear you.'

Wesley's Journal, 22 June 1736

He also made an enemy of Mrs Hawkins, one of the women who had prompted Charles's departure from Frederica. Upon visiting her at home, she attacked him with a pair of scissors, threatening first to kill him, and then to cut off his hair. She had to be pulled off Wesley by her husband, and the whole thing was witnessed by a crowd of people who heard a commotion and ran into the house.

A Frustrated Missionary

Wesley's stated aim in sailing to America had been to go amongst and preach to the Native American tribes, but he met with even less success here than he did as a pastor. Oglethorpe repeatedly refused to sanction a trip into the interior, claiming 'You cannot leave Savannah without a minister' (Wesley's Journal, 23 November 1736), and warning him he would most likely be killed by the French if he attempted to leave the colony. The nearest Wesley came to preaching to the Indians was when a group of warriors from the Chicasaw tribe came to Savannah, and he managed to secure an interview with them. Their conversation shows how tantalisingly open to the gospel the tribes might have been, if only they would have stopped warring amongst themselves.

Discussion with the Chicasaw Tribe

Q. Do you believe there is One above who is over all things?
A. *We believe there are four beloved things above: the clouds, the sun, the clear sky, and He that lives in the clear sky.*

Q. Do you believe there is but One that lives in the clear sky?

A. *We believe there are Two with Him, Three in all.*

Q. Do you think He made the sun, and other beloved things?

A. *We cannot tell. Who hath seen?*

Q. Do you think He made you?

A. *We think He made all men at first.*

Q. How do you think He made them at first?

A. *Out of the ground.*

Q. Do you believe He loves you?

A. *I do not know. I cannot see Him. . . .*

Q. We have a book that tells us many things of the beloved ones above; would you be glad to know them?

A. *We have no time now but to fight. If we should ever be at peace, we should be glad to know.*

Wesley's Journal, 20 July 1736

An Indecisive Lover

One of Wesley's few successful areas of Christian ministry in Georgia was with a small group in Savannah. Most of the congregation were indifferent to his message, but a handful was interested in learning and applying his own devotional rules. He invited this small group to join him in his house for further instruction after the Sunday services. One of their number was a pretty 18-year-old girl named Sophia Hopkey.

Wesley was impressed by this young lady's desire for spiritual knowledge, and the respect with which she listened to him and took his advice. But he soon found that his spiritual concern for her as a pastor was growing into a strong attraction to her as a woman. This was a problem for him on two counts. Firstly, he had decided that a Christian minister should be single in order to devote all his attention to serving God. Secondly, Sophia was already partially engaged to someone else – a young man named Thomas Mellichamp had proposed to her. Sophia lived with her uncle, Mr Causton, who was also the chief magistrate of Savannah. Seemingly, out of a desire for her to move out, Causton had agreed to her marrying Mellichamp, even though Mellichamp was known to be a bad character – so much so that he was put in prison for fraud. Sophia therefore found herself reluctantly engaged to a man in prison.

For Wesley, this became a licence to continue growing closer to Sophia. He believed that because of his commitment to a single life, and her confused engagement, the two would be protected from falling in love with each other. In reality, their feelings ran on ahead to something that was considerably more than spiritual friendship. In this they were encouraged by both Causton and Oglethorpe. Causton realized that Wesley was interested in his niece, and quickly decided that he would be a better catch for Sophia than the imprisoned Mellichamp. Oglethorpe was worried that Wesley would leave the colony to become a missionary to the native tribes and saw marriage as a way of tying Wesley down to a future in Georgia. Therefore, Oglethorpe arranged for Sophia to be Wesley's sole adult companion – apart from the crew on the boat – on a journey from Frederica back to Savannah.

Boat Journey to Savannah,

[26 October] In the evening we landed on an uninhabited island, made a fire, supped, went to prayers together, and then spread our sail over us on four stakes, to keep off the night dews. Under this on one side were Miss Sophy, myself, and one of our boys who came with me from Savannah; on the other, our boat's crew. The north-east wind was high and piercingly cold, and it was the first night she had ever spent in such a lodging. But she complained of nothing, appearing as satisfied as if she had been warm upon a bed of down.

[29 October] Observing in the night, the fire we lay by burning bright, that Miss Sophy was broad awake, I asked her, 'Miss Sophy, how far are you engaged to Mr Mellichamp?' She answered, 'I have promised him either to marry him or to marry no one at all.' I said (which indeed was the expression of a sudden wish, not of any formal design), 'Miss Sophy, I should think myself happy if I was to spend my life with you.' She burst out into tears and said, 'I am every way unhappy. I won't have Tommy; for he is a bad man. And I can have none else.' She added, 'Sir, you don't know the danger you are in. I beg you would speak no word more on this head.'

Wesley's Journal,
26–29 October 1736

When they returned to Savannah, Sophia spent each night at home with the Caustons, but was at Wesley's house in time for breakfast, and spent most of her days there. Wesley wrestled all through the winter of 1736–37 on whether to marry her or not. 'My desire and design to was still to live single; but how long it would continue I knew not' (Wesley's Journal, 1 November 1736). The Moravians advised him to marry, but Ingham and Delamotte were horrified by the idea he might marry someone so young, of whom he knew so little. He went away for a couple of days of retreat and prayer, and came back resolved that if he were to marry it would only be after he had fulfilled his mission to the Indian tribes. He told Sophia this in February 1737, and the very next day she stopped coming to his house for breakfast and dinner. But now he found that he missed her company terribly:

Calling at Mrs Causton's she was there alone. This was indeed an hour of trial. Her words, her eyes, her air, her every motion and gesture, were full of such a softness and sweetness! I knew not what might have been the consequence had I then but touched her hand. And how I avoided it I know not. Surely God is over all!

Wesley's Journal,
26 February 1737

By now he was again in turmoil over what to do, so he and Delamotte resolved to decide the matter once and for all by casting lots, a practice they had picked up from the Moravians in Georgia.

Deciding Whether to Marry

Having both of us sought God by deep consideration, fasting, and prayer, in the afternoon we conferred together, but could not come to any decision. We both apprehended Mr Ingham's objection to be the strongest, the doubt whether she was what she appeared. But this doubt was too hard for us to solve. At length we agreed to appeal to the Searcher of hearts. I accordingly made three lots. In one was writ 'Marry'; in the second, 'Think not of it this year.' After we had prayed to God 'to give a perfect lot,' Mr Delamotte drew the third, in which were the words, 'Think of it no more.' Instead of the agony I had reason to expect, I was enabled to say cheerfully, 'Thy will be done.' We cast lots once again to know whether I ought to converse with her any more; and the direction I received from God was, 'Only in the presence of Mr Delamotte.'

Wesley's Journal,
4 March 1737

However, another factor had come into play that would bring the relationship to a crisis point. It was rumoured that a new young man in the colony named William Williamson had been taking an interest in Sophia too. Wesley asked Sophia if there was anything going on between them. She told him there was nothing, and that she would never take an important decision without consulting Wesley first. One week later she was married to Williamson.

Sophia Hopkey's Marriage

About ten I called on Mrs Causton. She said, 'Sir, Mr Causton and I are exceedingly obliged to you for all the pains you have taken about Sophy. And so is Sophy too; and she desires you would publish the banns of marriage between her and Mr Williamson on Sunday.' She added, 'Sir, you don't seem to be well pleased. Have you any objection to it?' I answered, 'Madam, I don't seem to be awake. Surely I am in a dream.' She said, 'They agreed on it last night between themselves after you was gone. And afterwards Mr Williamson asked Mr Causton's and my consent, which we gave to him; but if you have any objection to it, pray speak. Speak to her. She is at the Lot. Go to her. She will be very glad to hear anything Mr Wesley has to say. . . .'

Soon after Mr Delamotte came back I went. Mr Williamson and she were together . . . silence ensued, which Mr Williamson broke thus: 'I suppose, sir, you know what was agreed on last night between Miss Sophy and me.' I answered, 'I have heard something; but I could not believe it, unless I should hear it from Miss Sophy herself.' She replied, 'Sir, I have given Mr Williamson my consent – unless you have anything to object.' It started into my mind, 'What if she means, unless you will marry me?' But I checked the thought with, 'Miss Sophy is so sincere: if she meant so, she would say so'; and replied, 'If you have given your consent, the time is past; I have nothing to object.' Mr Williamson desired me, if I had, to speak, and then left her and me together. 'Tis hard to describe the complication of passions and tumult of thought which I then felt: fear of her approaching misery, and tender pity; grief for my own loss; love shooting through all the recesses of my soul, and sharpening every thought and passion. Underneath there was a faint desire to do and suffer the will of God, which, joined to a doubt whether that proposal would be accepted, was just strong enough to prevent my saying plainly (what I wonder to this hour I did not say), 'Miss Sophy, will you marry me?'

She came to my house after evening prayers. Mr Williamson begged her not to stay after the rest of the company. But she did very readily. He walked to and fro on the outside of the house, with all the signs of strong uneasiness. I told her, 'Miss Sophy, you said yesterday you would take no steps in anything of importance without first consulting me.' She answered earnestly and many times over, 'Why, what could I do? I can't live in that house. I can't bear these shocks. This is quite a sudden thing. I have no particular inclination for Mr Williamson. I only promised if no objection appeared. But what can I do?' Mr Williamson, coming in abruptly, took her away, and put a short end to our conversation. . . .

The next morning she set out for Purrysburg, and on Saturday, March 12, 1737, was married there.

Wesley's Journal, 9 March 1737

A Wanted Man

Wesley was devastated by Sophia's actions. He considered refusing communion to her at church, since she had deceived him, and was only persuaded by Delamotte not to do this. On 5 July he wrote to her, accusing her of lying to him both regarding her feelings for Mellichamp and her relationship with Williamson. Just six days later the newly pregnant Mrs Williamson miscarried, and many in the Savannah community blamed Wesley due to the distress his letter had caused.

A month later Sophia made her next appearance at church, and this time Wesley did refuse to serve her communion: 'I repelled Mrs Williamson from the Holy Communion (for the reasons specified in my letter of July 5, as well as for not giving me notice of her design to communicate after having intermitted it for some time)' (Wesley's Journal, 7 August 1737). The next day an arrest warrant was issued against Wesley 'to answer the complaint of William Williamson and Sophia his wife, for defaming the said Sophia, and refusing to administer to her the Sacrament of the Lord's Supper, in a public congregation, without cause; by which the said William Williamson is damaged one thousand pounds sterling' (Wesley's Journal, 8 August 1737).

On 9 August 1737 Wesley was arrested, carried before magistrates, and told he must appear at the next court session held in Savannah. On 22 August the case began, but the hostile Causton adjourned court in his role as chief magistrate, and continued to delay the proceedings. A bill against Wesley was finally presented, alleging that he wrote to Sophia without Williamson's consent, but the trial continued to be deferred. Wesley turned up for his trial several times, only to be told to come back another day. It was in September that he first considered returning to England. On 22 November, Wesley told Causton he planned to leave soon, and posted up a notice in the town square to that effect. In early December he finally left the colony, as a wanted man with charges still against him.

Wesley Leaves Georgia

About ten the magistrates sent for me, and told me I must not go out of the province; for I had not answered the allegations laid out against me. I replied, 'I have appeared at six or seven Courts successively in order to answer them. But I was not suffered so to do, when I desired it time after time.' . . .

In the afternoon the magistrates published an order, requiring all the officers and sentinels to prevent my going out of the province, and forbidding any person to assist me so to do. Being now only a prisoner at large, in a place where I knew by experience every day would give fresh opportunity to procure evidence of words I never said, and actions I never did; I saw clearly the hour was come for me to fly for my life, leaving this place; and as soon as evening prayers were over, about eight o'clock, the tide then serving, I shook off the dust of my feet, and left Georgia.

Wesley's Journal, 2 December 1737

It took Wesley ten days to walk from Savannah to the port of Charlestown, the first few nights of which he and three other men lived as fugitives, sleeping in fields, living off a gingerbread cake, and digging in the ground each night to find water. On 22 December 1737 he boarded the *Samuel* and sailed for England.

Return as a Failure

Wesley had sailed to America with high hopes of converting the Native American tribes to Christianity. In so doing, he hoped to perfect his own relationship with God, believing strict holiness to be the way to salvation and peace with God. As things turned out, he was frustrated in his attempts to reach the native tribes and disillusioned with his work as a pastor. With his ministry in Georgia having been a failure, his personal relationships having been a disaster, and finally, with him being arrested and called to stand trial, he returned home feeling brokenhearted, spiritually bankrupt, and further from God than ever before. The danger of another Atlantic crossing, and the fears he experienced in the storms, left him dejected, and longing for a greater experience of God.

Thoughts when Returning to England

[24 January 1738] I went to America, to convert the Indians; but oh, who shall convert me? who, what is he that will deliver me from this evil heart of unbelief? I have a fair summer religion. I can talk well; nay, and believe myself, while no danger is near. But let death look me in the face, my spirit is troubled. Nor can I say, 'To die is gain'!

[1 February 1738] The faith I want is 'a sure trust and confidence in God, that, through the merits of Christ, my sins are forgiven, and I reconciled to the favour of God.' I want that faith which St Paul recommends to all the world, especially in his epistle to the Romans: that faith which enables every one that hath it to cry out, 'I live not; but Christ liveth in me; and the life which I now live, I live by faith in the Son of God, who loved me, and gave Himself for me.'

Wesley's Journal

The Failed Missionary

Key learning points

Spiritual Formation

Beware of confusing spiritual friendship with romance. With Sophia Hopkey, as with Sally Kirkham before, Wesley believed he could maintain a close, purely spiritual friendship with a woman, but later realized he had fallen in love.

Clear decisions are needed in relationships. Wesley struggled in deciding whether to marry Sophia, and then constantly changed his mind when the decision was made, causing confusion and heartache for both of them.

Treat people with integrity. Never use power to abuse or discriminate against others.

Learn from failure. Failure can teach valuable lessons. It can also draw us closer to God and help us realize our dependence on him. The only complete failures are those we choose to learn nothing from.

Leadership Skills

Clarify expectations. The different expectations of Oglethorpe and Wesley regarding Wesley's role in Georgia led to confusion and division down the line. If Wesley had clarified his roles and responsibilities at the beginning of the mission, there would have been less conflict later.

4

Finding a Life's Vocation

1738–39

Wesley arrived back in England just as his former Oxford friend George Whitefield was sailing out to America. Whitefield had answered a call from Wesley for more missionaries to come to Georgia, and ended up spending some time in Savannah as pastor of Wesley's old church. Although they missed each other on this occasion, the two would, over the next two years, plant the seeds of a British Evangelical Revival.

Peter Bohler

On arriving back in England, Wesley headed to London and quickly became friends with another group of Moravians, who were en route from Germany to serve as missionaries in America. He was again convicted of his lack of faith by their sure belief, and began to spend time talking with one of their members, Peter Bohler. Bohler recognized Wesley's zeal for holiness and piety, but also his need for a simpler faith that trusted in Christ for atonement, rather than on all his own good works. To Wesley's confusion, he plainly told him, 'My brother, my brother, that philosophy of yours must be purged away' (Wesley's Journal, 18 February 1738).

Bohler taught Wesley that salvation was only received through faith in Christ, rather than through good works, and that faith was a gracious gift from God, not something that Wesley could create through all his spiritual exercises. In a piece of classic advice, he then encouraged Wesley to continue preaching, and to actually begin preaching this new message of salvation through faith.

Bohler's Advice to Wesley on Preaching

Immediately it struck into my mind, 'Leave off preaching. How can you preach to others, who have not faith yourself?' I asked Bohler whether he thought I should leave it off or not. He answered, 'By no means.' I asked, 'But what can I preach?' He said, 'Preach faith *till* you have it; and then, *because* you have it, you *will* preach faith.'

Accordingly, Monday the 6th, I began preaching this new doctrine, though my soul started back from the work. The first person to whom I offered salvation by faith alone was a prisoner under sentence of death. His name was Clifford. Peter Bohler had many times desired me to speak to him before. But I could not prevail on myself so to do; being still (as I had been many years) a zealous assertor of the impossibility of a death-bed repentance.

Wesley's Journal, 4 March 1738

Wesley took the advice and continued to preach faith, both at church services, where he was invited to preside, and at the many religious society meetings that took place across London. At the church services this message of salvation through faith alone was not popular, since it carried an implication that most church members were not saved and needed to receive faith. Most churches were offended by this, and Wesley often found that his first invitation to preach at a particular church was also his last. By contrast, the various religious societies that often met in homes were excited to hear that salvation was so simple and so freely available. Wesley found himself more and more in demand as a speaker at these venues.

Meanwhile, he continued to discuss the nature of faith with the Moravians. Bohler showed him from the Bible that faith was the sole condition for salvation, and also that Christians could have an assurance of this salvation through a peace in their hearts, brought by the Holy Spirit. Wesley realized it was exactly this peace and assurance he was lacking, and for which he had been looking so long. Bohler then brought him Christians who testified that they had received this peace from God. Wesley wrote: 'I asked Peter Bohler again whether I ought not refrain from teaching others. He said, "No; do not hide in the earth the talent God hath given to you"' (Wesley's Journal, 22 April 1738).

Wesley's First Society

Bohler and the other London Moravians had drawn a substantial following, so he suggested that they start a society of their own, to support and disciple the new believers. They did this in May 1738 and the group came to be known as the Fetter Lane Society. Bohler himself was due to leave for America just a few days after their first meeting, and his command of English was still not fluent (he and Wesley spoke to each other in Latin) so the leadership passed on mainly to Wesley.

Rules of the Fetter Lane Society

This evening our little society began, which afterwards met in Fetter Lane. Our fundamental rules were as follows:

In obedience to the command of God by St James, and by the advice of Peter Bohler, it is agreed by us,

1. That we will meet together once a week to 'confess our faults one to another, and pray for one another, that we may be healed.'
2. That the persons so meeting be divided into several bands, or little companies, none of them consisting of fewer than five or more than ten persons.
3. That every one in order speak as freely, plainly, and concisely as he can, the real state of his heart, with his several temptations and deliverances, since the last time of meeting.
4. That all the bands have a conference at eight every Wednesday evening, begun and ended with singing and prayer.
5. That any who desire to be admitted into the society will be asked, 'What are your reasons for desiring this? Will you be entirely open; using no kind of reserve? Have you any objection to any of our orders?' (which may then be read)

6. That when any new member is proposed, every one present speak clearly and freely whatever objection he has to him.

7. That those against whom no reasonable objection appears be, in order for their trial, formed into one or more distinct bands, and some person agreed on to assist them.

8. That after two months' trial, if no objection then appear, they may be admitted into the society.

9. That every fourth Saturday be observed as a day of general intercession.

10. That on the Sunday seven-night following be a general love-feast, from seven till ten in the evening.

11. That no particular member be allowed to act in anything contrary to any order of the society; and that if any persons, after being thrice admonished, do not conform thereto, they be not any longer esteemed as members.

Wesley's Journal, 1 May 1738

The Fetter Lane Society may have been set up on the advice of Bohler, but from the beginning its clearly laid out rules, and its emphasis on members examining themselves, confessing sins to each other, and holding each other accountable, were definitely Wesleyan. The questions that each band member was to ask the other members at their weekly meetings were also clearly shaped by his awareness of the need for accountability through community in a religious movement.

Band Questions

1. What known sins have you committed since our last meeting?
2. What temptations have you met with?
3. How were you delivered?
4. What have you thought, said, or done, of which you doubt whether it be sin or not?

Taken from Rules of the Fetter Lane Society,
published 25 December 1738[1]

Wesley's 'Conversion'

Wesley was still searching for his peace with God when the Fetter Lane Society began on 1 May 1738, but he did not have long to wait. His brother Charles was with him in London at this time, and Charles too had been learning from Bohler about the doctrine of salvation by faith. He had been initially resistant, but now he was coming to a greater understanding: 'My brother had a long and particular conversation with Peter Bohler. And now it pleased God to open his eyes; so that he also saw clearly what was the nature of that one true living faith, whereby alone, "through grace we are saved"' (Wesley's Journal, 3 May 1738). On 21 May 1738 Charles found 'rest to his soul' (Wesley Journal, 19 May 1738), and three days later Wesley finally received the peace and certainty of faith that the Moravians had been telling him about, when his heart was 'strangely warmed'.

Wesley's Experience of God

[24 May] In the evening I went very unwillingly to a society in Aldersgate Street, where one was reading Luther's preface to the *Epistle to the Romans*. About a quarter before nine, while he was describing the change which God works in the heart through faith in Christ, I felt my heart strangely warmed. I felt I did trust in Christ, Christ alone for salvation; and an assurance was given me that He had taken away *my* sins, even *mine*, and saved *me* from the law of sin and death . . .

After my return home, I was much buffeted with temptations; but cried out, and they fled away. They returned again and again. I as often lifted up my eyes, and He 'sent me help from his holy place.' And herein I found the difference between this and my former state chiefly consisted. I was striving, yea, fighting with all my might under the law, as well as under grace. But then I was sometimes, if not often, conquered; now, I was always conqueror.

[25 May] The moment I awaked, 'Jesus, Master,' was in my heart and in my mouth; and I found all my strength lay in keeping my eye fixed upon Him, and my soul waiting on Him continually.

[27 May] Believing one reason of my want of joy was want of time for prayer, I resolved to do no business till I went to church in the morning, but to continue pouring out my heart before Him. And this day my spirit was enlarged; so that though I was now also assaulted by many temptations, I was more than conqueror, gaining

> more power thereby to trust and to rejoice in God my
> Saviour.
>
> *Wesley's Journal, 24–27 May 1738*

Here at last was the culmination of the spiritual search
that Wesley had begun back in Oxford in 1725, when his
mother had urged him to examine himself and see if he
really did have a 'reasonable hope of salvation'. All of
his actions since then – his constant self-examination
through his diary, his zeal for spiritual disciplines, his
strict Oxford rules, and even his ill-fated mission trip to
Georgia – had all been part of his search for salvation
and peace with God. Now he found that these things
came from the gift of faith. From now on he would continue with his zeal for God – his early rising to pray, his
using every moment of the day for spiritual pursuits –
but now it was all done out of love and desire for Jesus,
rather than an attempt to gain his favour. If it was a conversion, it was a conversion of belief rather than activity
– a conversion of the heart, just as Thomas à Kempis had
spoken to him all those years ago. Two weeks after this
Aldersgate experience, he sailed to Germany and spent
three months at Herrnhut, the spiritual home of the
Moravian community from whom he had learned so
much.

London Ministry

When Wesley returned to London, he spent his time
encouraging the Fetter Lane Society in their faith, in
preaching at the churches and other society meetings

where he was invited, and also in a renewed prison ministry, offering faith and salvation to those about to be executed:

> On Wednesday my brother and I went, at their earnest desire, to do the last good office to the condemned malefactors. It was the most glorious instance I ever saw of faith triumphing over sin and death. One observing the tears run fast down the cheeks of one of them in particular, while his eyes were steadily fixed upwards, a few moments before he died, asked, 'How do you feel your heart now?' He calmly replied, 'I feel a peace which I could not have believed to be possible. And I know it is the peace of God, which passeth all understanding.'
>
> *Wesley's Journal, 5 November 1738*

On 12 December 1738 Wesley met with a newly returned George Whitefield, who had just come back from America. Whitefield had undergone a similar conversion of the heart, and also a realization that the gift of faith was the key to a vibrant relationship with God. He had become a powerful speaker, and was passionately preaching evangelistic messages to all the churches and societies who would hear him. He became a close friend and ally of the Fetter Lane Society.

New Year's Eve 1738

Mr Hall, Kinchin, Ingham, Whitefield, Hutchins, and my brother Charles were present at our lovefeast in Fetter

Lane, with about sixty of our brethren. About three in the morning, as we were continuing instant in prayer, the power of God came mightily upon us, insomuch that many cried out for exceeding joy, and many fell to the ground. As soon as we were recovered a little from that awe and amazement at the presence of His majesty we broke out with one voice, 'We praise Thee, O God; we acknowledge Thee to be the Lord.'

Wesley's Journal, 1 January 1739

Open-air Preaching

At this point Wesley and Whitefield were spending much of their time preaching at the different London society meetings, but now Whitefield proposed they went one step further. They both had a passion for sharing the message of salvation with as many as possible, and Whitefield realized they could not do this in church meetings. Whitefield suggested preaching in public places, where people already were, in order to reach the masses.

Wesley had deep reservations – a clergyman preaching outdoors was unheard of. They prayed together 'that nothing may be done rashly' (George Whitefield's Journal, 24 January 1739).[2] Whitefield then set out for a preaching tour of his native West Country. However, in March 1739 he wrote to Wesley, pressing him to come and join him in Bristol as soon as possible. When Wesley arrived he found that Whitefield had been so moved by the sight of working-class people, living in poverty and without knowing the gospel, he had begun preaching to the local coal miners of Kingswood, a Bristol suburb. The miners had begun listening to him on their way to work, and many were responding to the message. But, since Whitefield was due to sail back across the Atlantic for another preaching tour of America, he needed Wesley to set up a society for discipling the miners, and to continue the open-air preaching. Wesley was apprehensive, but could see the impact the work was having on the miners, and so reluctantly took on the responsibility.

First Sermons Outside

[31 March] In the evening I reached Bristol, and met Mr Whitefield there. I could scarce reconcile myself at first to this strange way of preaching in the fields, of which he set me an example on Sunday; having been all my life (till very lately) so tenacious of every point relating to decency and order, that I should have thought the saving of souls almost a sin if it had not been done in a church.

[1 April] In the evening, Mr Whitefield being gone, I began expounding our Lord's Sermon on the Mount (one pretty remarkable precedent of field-preaching, though I suppose there were churches at that time also) to a little society which was accustomed to meet once or twice a week in Nicholas Street.

[2 April] At four in the afternoon I submitted to be more vile, and proclaimed in the highways the glad tidings of salvation, speaking from a little eminence in a ground adjoining to the city, to about three thousand people. The scripture on which I spoke was this (is it possible any one should be ignorant that it is fulfilled in every true minister of Christ?), 'The Spirit of the Lord is upon Me, because He hath anointed Me to preach the gospel to the poor. He hath sent Me to heal the broken hearted; to preach deliverance to the captives, and recovery of sight to the blind; to set at liberty them that are bruised, to proclaim the acceptable year of the Lord.'

Wesley's Journal

A Wesleyan society was set up in Bristol, and a second in Kingswood, both operating with the same rules as the London Fetter Lane Society. (A school was also set up to educate the children of the miners in Kingswood.) Wesley would eventually take this model of field-preaching and societies across the British Isles, but although he would become one of the greatest champions of field-preaching in church history, his Anglican high churchmanship never sat happily with it. He persisted not because he enjoyed it, but because he realized it was the best way for him to reach the largest number of people with the gospel.

Wesley on Field-Preaching

[20 May 1759] Oh what a victory Satan would gain if he could put an end to field-preaching! But that, I trust, he never will; at least not till my head is laid.

[23 June 1759] On Monday and Tuesday evening I preached abroad, near the Keelman's Hospital, to twice the people we should have had at the house. What marvel the devil does not love field-preaching? Neither do I: I love a commodious room, a soft cushion, a handsome pulpit. But where is my zeal if I do not trample all these under foot in order to save one more soul?

[6 September 1772] I preached on the quay, at Kingswood, and near King's Square. To this day field-preaching is a cross to me. But I know my commission and see no other way of 'preaching the gospel to every creature.'

Wesley's Journal

An Apostolic Ministry

Wesley quickly settled into a routine of preaching at different open-air meeting points in and around Bristol, travelling in a circuit even as far away as Bath. He would preach each weekday morning at 5 a.m. to reach coal miners and others on their way to work. In the afternoon he would speak to crowds on their way home, and at the weekends to groups who would gather in public parks and common areas. He would then encourage the converts at the regular society meetings that began to take place under his direction. Due to this itinerant ministry, he often used the same sermons in different venues, and messages such as, 'It is by grace you are saved, through faith', 'This sect which is everywhere talked against', 'Almost thou persuadest me to become a Christian', 'Why will ye die, O house of Israel', 'Christ the wisdom of God' and 'What does it profit a man to gain the whole world, if he loses his soul' could be heard all across Bristol and the surrounding area in 1739. He continued to defend reusing his sermons throughout his life and ministry.

Wesley on Reusing Sermons

I went to Tiverton. I was musing here on what I heard a good man say long since – 'Once in seven years I burn all my sermons; for it is a shame if I cannot write better sermons now than I could seven years ago.' Whatever others can do, I really cannot. I cannot write a better sermon on the Good Steward than I did seven years ago; I cannot write a better on the Great Assize than I did twenty years ago; I cannot write a better on the Use of Money, than I did nearly thirty years ago; nay, I know not that I can write a better on the Circumcision of the Heart than I did five-and-forty years ago. Perhaps, indeed, I may have read five or six hundred books more than I had then, and may know a little more history, or natural philosophy, than I did; but I am not sensible that this has made any essential addition to my knowledge in divinity.

Wesley's Journal, 1 September 1778

Having successfully introduced Wesley to the public of Kingswood, Whitefield did the same in London at Blackheath before he left for America. Later on, both preachers also spoke at Kennington Common, and at Moorfields, just north of the city. Wesley began dividing his time between London and Bristol, preaching in the public areas and building up the societies. Whilst evangelistic preaching was something both men had in common, the forming of societies came to be a distinction between their ministries. Whitefield was a great preacher, rather than an organizer, and did little to follow up his converts' spiritual progress. Early in their ministry he criticized Wesley for founding societies, but later on remarked, 'My brother Wesley acted wisely – the souls that were awakened under his ministry he joined in class, and thus preserved the fruit of his labour. This I neglected, and my people are a rope of sand.'[3]

By contrast, Wesley had always been convinced of the need for new converts to be gathered together into societies and bands for continued growth, and he became more convicted of his position later in life.

Wesley on Founding Societies

I was more convinced than ever that the preaching like an apostle, without joining together those that are awakened and training them up in the ways of God, is only begetting children for the murderer. How much preaching has there been for these twenty years all over Pembrokeshire! But no regular societies, no discipline, no order or connexion; and the consequence is that nine in ten of the once-awakened are now faster asleep than ever.

Wesley's Journal, 25 August 1763

Anglican Opposition

However, not everybody was supportive of this new ministry. The Anglican Church tolerated extra religious societies (such as the Fetter Lane congregation) to be set up within its structure, but they were rarely led by clergymen, since this undermined the authority of the local parish minister. Even prior to his decision to preach in the fields, Wesley was therefore considered a troublemaker by some sections of his church, and was compelled to write a defence of his ministry that contained one of his most famous slogans.

Wesley's Parish

God in Scripture commands me, according to my power, to instruct the ignorant, reform the wicked, confirm the virtuous. Man forbids me to do this in another's parish: that is, in effect, to do it at all; seeing I have now no parish of my own, nor probably ever shall. Whom, then, shall I hear, God or man? 'If it be just to obey man rather than God, judge you. A dispensation of the gospel is committed to me; and woe is me if I preach not the gospel.' But where shall I preach it, upon the principles you mention? Why, not in Europe, Asia, Africa, or America; not in any of the Christian parts, at least, of the habitable earth: for all these are, after a sort, divided into parishes. . . .

Suffer me now to tell you my principles in this matter. *I look upon all the world as my parish*; thus far I mean, that in whatever part of it I am I judge it meet, right, and my bounden duty to declare, unto all that are willing to hear, the glad tidings of salvation. This is the work which I know God has called me to; and sure I am that his blessing attends it.

Letter from John Wesley to James Hervey,
20 March 1739 [italics added][4]

Initial church opposition to Wesley and Whitefield came to a head in August 1739, after five months of work amongst the miners of Bristol. Wesley was summoned to a meeting with the Bishop of Bristol, who had become alarmed through reports of this new, seditious ministry that was undermining the traditional structures of the Church of England. Wesley reminded the bishop that as an ordained man he was free to preach wherever he felt called.

Arguing with the Bishop of Bristol

Bishop: Mr Wesley, I will deal plainly with you. I once thought you and Mr Whitefield well-meaning men; but I cannot think so now. For I have heard more of you: matters of fact, sir. And Mr Whitefield says in his Journal: 'There are promises still to be fulfilled in me.' Sir, the pretending to extraordinary revelations and gifts of the Holy Ghost is a horrid thing – a very horrid thing!

Wesley: My lord, for what Mr Whitefield says Mr Whitefield, and not I, is accountable. I pretend to no extraordinary revelations, or gifts of the Holy Ghost: none but what every Christian may receive and ought to expect and pray for. . . .

Bishop: Well, sir, since you ask my advice, I will give it you very freely. You have no business here; you are not commissioned to preach in this diocese. Therefore I advise you to go hence.

Wesley: My lord, my business on earth is to do what good I can. Wherever, therefore, I think I can do most good there must I stay, so long as I think so. At present I think I can do most good here; therefore here I stay. As to my

> preaching here, a dispensation of the gospel is committed
> to me, and woe is me if I preach not the gospel wherever I
> am in the habitable world!
>
> *Wesley's Journal, 18 August 1739*

Wesley could therefore still claim to be working within the Anglican Church, but he was clear that from now on he would follow God and his own conscience, rather than any rules the church would attempt to place him under.

Two events within two years had set the course for the remainder of Wesley's life. His contact with the Moravians and his experience at Aldersgate taught him that salvation came by faith alone, and that each Christian could know the presence of God in their own life. His contact with Whitefield then led him to begin preaching this message to the unchurched masses, and to follow up this preaching through forming and regulating societies. He had a message, and he had a medium for getting that message across. He was 35, and would devote the remaining fifty-three years of his life to this work.

Finding A Life's Vocation

Key learning points

Spiritual Formation

Experience God. Before meeting Jesus personally, Wesley saw little fruit in his ministry. Afterwards, his relationship with Christ changed his impact upon the world.

Find a spiritual mentor. Wesley was not ashamed to talk with, and learn from, Bohler and the other Moravians who had a deeper relationship with God than his own. What he learned from them was priceless.

Discerning Vision

Use gifts in discerning call. Where God calls, he also equips. Therefore, our skills can point back to our calling. By using his gift for preaching, Wesley discerned his life's calling of preaching faith to the masses. Doors opened up for him as he used his gift to serve the Lord.

Be part of a community. The fellowship of the Fetter Lane Society ensured they all shared ideas and supported each other in discerning God's will for each of them.

Opposition can help clarify vision. Dealing with the criticism of opponents helped Wesley in discerning and refining vision. The criticism levelled at his ministry led to his new understanding: 'I look upon all the world as my parish'.

Mission Skills

Go to where people are. Evangelism has to start with meeting people where they currently are, and then seeking to help them meet the Lord.

The same message can be relevant to many people. Both Wesley and Whitefield repeated the same sermon to many different groups of people, with powerful results.

Disciple converts. New believers need mature Christians to help them grow. Wesley took responsibility for creating societies and bands to disciple those who were converted.

5

Founding a Movement

1739–48

Having discerned his life work, Wesley spent the 1740s developing Methodism into a national movement. Internal splits and external riots could not stop the rise of a revival movement that was to develop across England, Wales and Ireland by the end of the decade.

Governance of Societies

In early 1740 Methodism was a growing movement, but only existing in two areas: Bristol and London. In these cities there were Methodist societies that had grown out of the field-preaching of Whitefield and the Wesley brothers, but it was Wesley who developed the rules and format for when and how the societies should meet. Since April 1739 Wesley had emphasized the importance of field-preaching, society meetings and band meetings to his followers. In February 1742 the first class meetings took place in Bristol. Six weeks later the London societies were also divided into classes, and the first Watch-Night services were held. By this point Methodist societies had developed the structure and meeting format they would use throughout Wesley's lifetime:

Many met together to consult on a proper method for discharging the public debt [in Bristol]; and it was at length agreed, (1) that every member of the society who was able should contribute a penny a week; (2) that the whole society should be divided into little companies or classes – about twelve in each class; and (3) that one person in each class should receive the contribution of the rest, and bring it in to the stewards, weekly.

Wesley's Journal, 15 February 1742

The Meetings of Methodist Societies

Methodist members were expected to attend all of the meetings listed below. Failure to do so could result in either Wesley or the local assistant removing people from membership.

Field-Preaching
Regular open-air preaching in public places, where all people could hear the gospel message. Wesley emphasized 5 a.m. on a weekday morning, to allow workers the chance to hear the message before they began the day's work. Field-preaching also occurred in the evenings, and at weekends in public parks.

Society Meeting
A weekly evening meeting for all society members, with hymn singing and preaching. Converts from field meetings were encouraged to join the local society meeting.

Anglican Church Attendance
Wesley wanted Methodism to be a renewing movement within the Church of England. Therefore, all Methodists were expected to attend their local parish church services on a Sunday – even if the local clergy were anti-Methodist – for fellowship, and to take communion.

Class Meetings
Although they began as a means for collecting money, the class meetings became a weekly Bible study for small groups of twelve members. Class leaders were pastorally responsible for the members of their classes.

Band Meetings
Weekly meetings for around three to five people of the same sex, who would ask each other the accountability questions listed in the previous chapter.

Watch-Night Services
Monthly prayer meetings, usually held on the Friday night nearest the full moon (so people had the moonlight to help them make their way home in the dark). They usually lasted around four hours, from 8 p.m. to just after midnight.

Love-Feasts
Usually held every three months, where society members gathered to share bread and water, and then testify about what God was doing in their lives.

Internal Opposition

Although there were only two centres of Methodism during these early years, both caused serious work for Wesley due to the internal divisions and splits they went through. Wesley now spent most of his time in and around Bristol, preaching, organizing societies, and overseeing the creation of the school at Kingswood. It was inevitable that his long absences from London would result in problems for the Fetter Lane congregation.

The Moravians dominated the leadership and preaching of Fetter Lane when Wesley was away. One prominent Moravian preacher called Philip Molther began to teach a doctrine known as 'stillness', which was based on the text 'Be still and know that I am God' (Ps. 46:10). Molther taught the members that they should wait patiently for God to give them faith, and should not pray, read the Bible, take Holy Communion, or even attempt to perform good works, for fear they should think these actions had saved them, rather than relying solely on the grace of God for salvation. In other words, they were asked to 'be still'.

With his strong emphasis on the means of grace (especially through prayer, Bible study and communion), Wesley seriously disagreed with this teaching. On his visits to London, he would remonstrate strongly against this passivity, but to little avail:

At eight our society met at Fetter Lane. We sat an hour without speaking. The rest of the time was spent in dispute, one having proposed a question concerning the Lord's Supper. . . .

> I observed every day more and more the advantage
> Satan had gained over us.
>
> *Wesley's Journal, 7 November 1739*

This continued for nine months, with Wesley continually attempting to persuade both the Moravian leaders and the Fetter Lane members that the means of grace were available to help build faith in God, and should not be put in opposition to faith. However, due to his long absences in Bristol, he could not prevail, and eventually on 20 July 1740 he read a paper at a Fetter Lane meeting explaining where he differed with them theologically, how he had tried repeatedly to turn them from their errors, and stating he would be leaving the congregation to the Moravians. Eighteen people left the meeting with him, and began a separate London Methodist society known as The Foundery. The separation with the Moravians, who had helped him so much on his own journey of faith and discernment, was now complete.

In Bristol there were also internal divisions to overcome, but these were due to disagreements over predestination rather than 'stillness'. Whitefield had become a strong Calvinistic predestinarian on a preaching tour of North America, and came back preaching the doctrine in England. Again, this brought a dispute with Wesley, a firm believer in the grace of God being available for all sinners. The colleagues discussed the matter, in person and through their letters, but attempted to keep their differences private, so as to preserve the unity of the revival movement.

Resolving Internal Divisions

A private letter, written to me by Mr Whitefield, was printed without either his leave or mine, and great copies were
given to our people. . . . I told them, 'I will do just what I
believe Mr Whitefield would do, were he here himself.'
Upon which I tore it to pieces before them all. Everyone
who had received it, did the same. So that in two minutes
there was not a whole copy left.

Wesley's Journal, 1 February 1741

Inevitably though, tensions would surface. The leading
predestinarian in Bristol, John Cennick, began to preach
personally against both Wesley brothers. This was too
much for Wesley. He could tolerate differences of opinion
over theology, but not insubordination from his preachers. Cennick, and some of his colleagues, were therefore
dismissed from the Bristol society in February 1741, 'not
for their opinions. . . . but for their scoffing at the Word
and ministers of God, for their tale-bearing, back-biting,
and evil speaking, for their dissembling, lying, and slandering' (Wesley's Journal, 28 February 1741).

Teamwork

Teamwork was one of the most important aspects of early
Methodism. In the 1740s Wesley gathered a very competent
team, with he and his brother sharing the leadership of the
societies between them: 'My brother and I agreed it was
enough for one of us to stay in town, while the other
endeavoured to strengthen our brethren in other parts'

(Wesley's Journal, 24 March 1744); 'My brother returned from the north, and I prepared to supply his place there' (Wesley's Journal, 10 February 1747).

It was due to teamwork that Methodism spread beyond Bristol and London. A Calvinistic Welsh preacher called Howell Harris began preaching and gathering converts into societies across south Wales. He then invited Wesley to come and preach in Wales. Similarly, a Yorkshire stonemason called John Nelson heard Wesley preach in London, and returned home to Birstall to preach the same message. Methodism became a true team endeavour, relying on the Wesley brothers and Whitefield (when he was in Britain) as national preachers who travelled around the country, while local leaders and preachers maintained societies, and often began new ones through their preaching tours. Support was also given to the movement from the upper classes by the Countess of Huntingdon, an early member of the Fetter Lane congregation, who provided financial support and opened doors to the aristocratic societies of London.

Wesley was astute enough to realize this, and to allow all the members of the team the opportunities to use their unique gifts. Whitefield was free to employ his dramatic oratory to win over the crowds, Charles was encouraged to use his evangelistic gifts, often taking the initial preaching tour when new societies were being formed. He also used his poetic skills to write the hymns that Methodists began singing at their meetings. Local leaders (usually laymen, rather than Anglican clergy) could then preach at the field and society meetings, lead classes and bands, and so become involved in the growing revival ministry.

Growth of Movement

With the internal divisions of the Bristol and London societies overcome, a tried and tested structure for local societies in place, and local leaders beginning to preach and gather societies together, Methodism began to expand across the country. Wesley was persuaded by

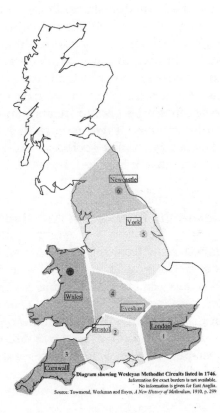

Diagram showing **Wesleyan Methodist Circuits listed in 1746.**
Information for exact borders is not available.
No information is given for East Anglia.
Source: Townsend, Workman and Eayrs, *A New History of Methodism*, 1910, p. 299

Howell Harris to make a short tour with him around Cardiff, Newport and Abergavenny in October 1741. There were also visits to Donnington, arranged by the Countess of Huntingdon, and to Yorkshire, to visit the societies of John Nelson. In May 1742 Wesley visited Newcastle for the first time, and made the city into a third base for the movement.

A national movement required further structures, and in 1744 the first Methodist conference took place. This laid down the rules which Methodist preachers were expected to abide by. At the 1746 conference the movement was organized into seven circuits (or preaching rounds): London, Bristol, Cornwall, Evesham, Yorkshire, Newcastle and Wales. Local preachers, or assistants, were expected to visit all of the societies included in their circuit. In 1747 Wesley made his first brief visit to Ireland, and followed this up with a longer stay of two months in 1748. By the end of the decade, Methodist societies could be found spread throughout most of England, Wales and Ireland.

What are the Rules of an Assistant?

1. Be diligent, never be unemployed a moment, never be triflingly employed, never while away time, spend no more time at any place than is strictly necessary.

2. Be serious. Let your motto be, 'Holiness unto the Lord.' Avoid all lightness as you would hell-fire, and laughing as you would cursing and swearing.

3. Touch no woman. Be as loving as you will, but hold your hands off 'em. Custom is nothing to us.

4. Believe evil of no one. If you see it done, well, else take heed how you credit it. Put the best construction on everything. You know the judge is always supposed to be on the prisoner's side.

5. Speak evil of no one, else your word especially would eat as doth a canker. Keep your thoughts within your own breast till you come to the person concerned.

6. Tell everyone what you think wrong in him, and that plainly, and as soon as may be, else it will fester in your own heart. Make all haste, therefore, to cast the fire out of your bosom.

7. Do nothing as a gentleman: you have no more to do with this character than with that of a dancing master. You are the servant of all, therefore. . . .

8. Be ashamed of nothing but sin: not of fetching wood, or drawing water, if time permit; not of cleaning your own shoes or your neighbours'.

9. Take no money of any one. If they give you food when you are hungry, or clothes when you need them, it is good. But not silver or gold. Let there be no pretence to say, 'we grow rich by the Gospel.'

10. Contract no debt without my knowledge.

11. Be punctual: do everything exactly at the time; and in general do not mend our rules, but keep them, not for wrath but for conscience sake.

12. Act in all things, not according to your own will, but as a son in the Gospel. As such, it is your part to employ your time in the manner which we direct: partly in visiting the flock from house to house (the sick in particular); partly, in such course of reading, meditation, and prayer, as we advise from time to

time. Above all, if you labour with us in our Lord's vineyard, it is needful you should do that part of the work which we prescribe at those times and places which we judge most for His glory.

You have nothing to do but to save souls. Therefore spend and be spent in this work. And go always, not only to those who want you, but to those who want you most.

Minutes of Conference,
29 June 1744, revised 1745[1]

Violent Opposition

Methodism's success of winning many converts from its open-air meetings, especially from the working classes, inevitably dragged it into conflicts. Early opposition took the form of hecklers attempting to shout down Wesley, or distract him with arguments whilst he preached. On more than one occasion his opponents tried to drive live animals (usually cows) into the crowds to disrupt meetings. Wesley could ignore such opposition – and was amused by the story of an attempted farce in Newcastle to discredit Methodism – but the opposition also became violent. Mud, stones and bricks were thrown regularly during field-preaching, and while Wesley himself could marvel at God's protection during such incidents, others were not so fortunate. As early as October 1740 Methodism received its first martyr when William Seward, on a preaching tour around Wales with Howell Harris, was killed by a fatal stone whilst preaching.

A Newcastle Play

The following advertisement was published:

FOR THE BENEFIT OF MR. ESTE,

By the Edinburgh Company of Comedians, on *Friday, November 4*, will be acted a Comedy called

THE CONSCIOUS LOVERS;

To which will be added a Farce, called,

TRICK UPON TRICK, or
METHODISM DISPLAYED.

On Friday a vast multitude of spectators were assembled in the Moot Hall to see this. It was believed there could not be less than fifteen hundred people, some hundreds of whom sat on rows of seats built upon the stage. Soon after the comedians had begun the first act of the play, on a sudden all those seats fell down at once, the supporters of them breaking like a rotten stick. The people were thrown one upon another, about five foot forward, but not one of them hurt. After a short time the rest of the spectators were quiet, and the actors went on. In the middle of the second act all the shilling seats gave a crack and sunk several inches down. A great noise and shrieking followed; and as many as could readily get to the door went out and returned no more. Notwithstanding this, when the noise was over, the actors went on with the play. In the beginning of the third act the entire stage suddenly sunk about six inches. The players retired with great precipitation; yet in a while they began again. At the latter end of the third act all the sixpenny seats, without any kind of notice, fell to the ground. There was now a cry on every side, it being supposed that many were crushed to pieces; but, upon inquiry, not a single person (such was the mercy of God!) was either killed or dangerously hurt. Two or three hundred remaining still in the hall, Mr. Este (who was to act the Methodist) came upon the stage and told them, for all this, he was resolved the farce should be acted. While he was speaking the stage sunk six inches more; on which he ran back in the utmost confusion, and the people as fast as they could out of the door, none staying to look behind him.

Which is most surprising – that those players acted this farce the next week, or that some hundreds of people came again to see it?

Wesley's Journal, 2 November 1743

Wesley's first experience of nearly being killed by a riotous mob came in Staffordshire in 1743, when he endured five hours of being assaulted in the streets. By then he and his lay preachers had become accustomed to being 'arrested' by local mobs, and dragged to the nearest magistrate's house by an enraged group, who then often realized they had no specific charges to bring against them. The experience below, from his home town of Epworth, is typical:

I rode over to a neighbouring town to wait upon a Justice of Peace, a man of candour and understanding; before whom (I was informed) their angry neighbours had carried a whole wagon-load of these new heretics. But when he asked what they had done there was a deep silence; for that was a point their conductors had forgot. At length one said, 'Why, they pretended to be better than other people; and, besides, they prayed from morning to night.' Mr. Stovin asked, 'But have they done nothing besides?' 'Yes, sir,' said an old man: 'an't please your worship, they have *converted* my wife. Till she went among them, she had such a tongue! And now she is as quiet as a lamb.' 'Carry them back, carry them back,' replied the Justice, 'and let them convert all the scolds in the town.'

Wesley's Journal, 9 June 1742

Staffordshire Riots

Before five the mob surrounded the house again in greater numbers than ever. The cry of one and all was, 'Bring out the minister; we will have the minister.' I desired one to take their captain by the hand and bring him into the house. After a few sentences interchanged between us the lion was become a lamb. I desired him to go and bring one or two more of the most angry of his companions. He brought in two, who were ready to swallow the ground with rage; but in two minutes they were as calm as he. I bade them make way, that I might go out among the people. As soon as I was in the midst of them I called for a chair, and, standing up, asked 'What do any of you want with me?' Some said, 'We want you to go with us to the Justice.' I replied, 'That I will, with all my heart.' I then spoke a few words, which God applied; so that they cried out with might and main, 'The gentleman is an honest gentleman, and we will spill our blood in his defence.' . . .

One or two ran before to tell Mr. Lane they had brought Mr. Wesley before his Worship. Mr. Lane replied, 'What have I to do with Mr. Wesley? Go and carry him back again.' By this time the main body came up, and began knocking at the door. A servant told them Mr. Lane was in bed. His son followed, and asked what was the matter. One replied, 'Why, an't please you, they sing psalms all day; nay, and make folks rise at five in the morning. And what would your Worship advise us to do?' 'To go home,' said Mr. Lane, 'and be quiet.' . . .

But we had not gone a hundred yards when the mob of Walsall came, pouring in like a flood, and bore down all before them. . . . To attempt to speak was vain, for the noise on every side was like the roaring of the sea. So they dragged me along till we came to the town, where, seeing the door of a large house open, I attempted to go in; but a man, catching me by the hair, pulled me back into the middle of the mob . . . I stood at the door and asked, 'Are you willing to hear me speak?' Many cried out, 'No, no! knock his brains out; down with him; kill him at once. . . .'

My strength and my voice returned, and I broke aloud into prayer. And now the man who just before headed the mob turned and said, 'Sir, I will spend my life for you: follow me, and not one soul here shall touch a hair of your head.' Two or three of his fellows confirmed his words, and got close to me immediately. . . . The people then, as if it had been by common consent, fell back to the right and left; while those three or four men took me between them, and carried me through them all. . . .

By how gentle degrees does God prepare us for his will! Two years ago a piece of brick grazed my shoulders. It was a year after that the stone struck me between the eyes. Last month I received one blow, and this evening two; one before we came into the town, and one after we were gone out.

Wesley's Journal, 20 October 1743

Wesley's tactics in Staffordshire, and in a later riot in Cornwall, were the same whenever he encountered violent mobs. When faced with a hostile crowd, he always stood his ground, looked individuals in the eye, and spoke to the leaders. His theory was to win the leaders over to him, and in that way win the crowd. He would repeatedly ask if he could speak, and whenever they let him he would preach the love of God to them.

Cornwall Riot

I rode to Falmouth. About three in the afternoon I went to see a gentlewoman who had been long indisposed. Almost as soon as I was set down, the house was beset on all sides by an innumerable multitude of people. A louder or more confused noise could hardly be at the taking of a city by storm. . . .

The rabble roared with all their throats, 'Bring out the Canorum! Where is the Canorum? (an unmeaning word which the Cornish generally use instead of Methodist).' No answer being given, they quickly forced open the outer door and filled the passage. . . .

Poor Kitty was utterly astonished, and cried out, 'O sir, what must we do?' I said, 'We must pray.' Indeed at that time, to all appearance, our lives were not worth an hour's purchase. She asked, 'But, sir, is it not better for you to hide yourself? To get into the closet? I answered, 'No. It is best for me to stand just where I am.' . . .

Away went all the hinges at once, and the door fell back into the room. I stepped forward at once into the midst of them, and said, 'Here I am. Which of you has anything to say to me? To which of you have I done any wrong? To you? Or you? Or you?' I continued speaking till I came, bare-headed as I was (for I purposely left my hat, that they might all see my face), into the middle of the street, and then, raising my voice, said, 'Neighbours, countrymen! Do you desire to hear me speak?' They cried vehemently, 'Yes, yes. He shall speak. He shall. Nobody shall hinder him.' But having nothing to stand on, and no advantage of ground, I could be heard by few only. However, I spoke with intermission, and, as far as the sound reached, the people were still; till one or two of their captains turned about and swore not a man should touch him.

Wesley's Journal, 4 July 1745

God's Protection in Bolton

There was a vast number of people, but many of them utterly wild. As soon as I began speaking they began thrusting to and fro, endeavouring to throw me down from the steps on which I stood. . . . They then began to throw stones . . . on which I could not but observe how God overrules even the minutest circumstances. One man was bawling just at my ear when a stone struck him on the cheek, and he was still. A second was forcing his way down to me, till another stone hit him on the forehead; it bounded back, the blood ran down, and he came no farther. The third, being close to me, stretched out his hand, and in the instant a sharp stone came upon the joints of his fingers; he shook his hand, and was very quiet till I concluded my discourse and went away.

Wesley's Journal, 28 August 1748

In Falmouth Wesley was in danger not simply because certain groups opposed his preaching, but because they supposed him to be in league with France and Spain (whom Britain was at war with at the time). Wesley's message that faith in God should lead to good works in people's lives was confused by some, who labelled him a Roman Catholic, accusing him of treason, and of supporting the Catholic European nations against Britain.

It was perhaps because of these accusations that Methodism's enemies came up with their greatest attempt for thwarting the movement. With Britain being at war with so many nations, new troops were constantly required for the army. It was illegal to conscript

Anglican priests, but the mobs could round up the Methodist lay preachers, claim that they were disturbing the peace with their preaching, and have them press-ganged into national service. Many of Wesley's best lay preachers, such as John Nelson, Thomas Maxfield from London, and Thomas Beard from Yorkshire suffered this fate. What better way to rid the country of Methodists, than to round up the leaders and send them to fight and die overseas?

However, even this could not stop the message. Preachers continued to speak and minister to the troops they marched with, and Methodist societies began to spring up in different regiments across the army. John Haime voluntarily enlisted into the army, became a Christian, and wrote to Wesley asking how he could be of service whilst abroad. Wesley encouraged him to preach to the troops, and he became one of Wesley's most effective helpers – both in the army and when he returned home.

John Haime's Army Ministry

We marched to the camp, near Brussels. There are a few of us joined into a society, being sensible, where two or three are gathered in His name, there is our Lord in the midst of them. Our place of meeting was a small wood near the camp. . . . Here I began to speak openly, at a small distance from the camp, just in the middle of the English army; and here it pleased God to give me some evidence that my labour was not in vain. We sung a hymn, which drew about two hundred soldiers together, and they all behaved decently. After I had prayed I began

to exhort them; and though it rained very hard, yet very
few went away. . . .

Our society is now increased to upwards of two hundred; and the hearers are frequently more than a thousand, although many say I am mad; and others have
endeavoured to incense the Field Marshal against us. I
have been sent for, and examined several times; but,
blessed be God, He has always delivered me. . . .

During our abode in the camp at Assche I have
preached thirty-five times in seven days . . . we meet at
eight in the morning, at three in the afternoon, and
seven at night; and commonly two whole nights in each
week. . . .

Your unworthy brother in the Lord, John Haime
Wesley's Journal, 4 November 1744

A soldier named John Evans was converted through
John Haime's ministry in the army, and he in turn
became one of Haime's greatest helpers until his death:
'[Evans] continued both to preach and to live the gospel
till the battle of Fontenoy. One of his companions saw
him there, laid across a cannon, both his legs having
been taken off by a chain-shot, praising God and exhort-
ing all that were round about him; which he did till his
spirit returned to God' (Wesley's Journal, 3 December
1744).

Method for Starting New Societies

John Haime's tactics for beginning a Methodist society
in his regiment were typical of how Methodism began

in a new town. To start a fresh society, one or two preachers would together visit an open area where people naturally congregated – a high street, a park, etc. – and sing a couple of hymns to draw a crowd. They would then pray, preach to those who had gathered out of curiosity – all the while hoping more would come – and at the end invite those interested in learning or hearing more to come again for further instruction. In this way societies began in army regiments, and in many towns of the British Isles.

Beginning the Society in Newcastle

Standing at the end of the street with John Taylor, [I] began to sing the hundredth Psalm. Three or four people came out to see what was the matter, who soon increased to four or five hundred. I suppose there might be twelve to fifteen hundred before I had done preaching. . . .

Observing the people, when I had done, to stand gaping and staring upon me with the most profound astonishment, I told them, 'If you desire to know who I am, my name is John Wesley. At five in the evening, with God's help, I design to preach here again.'

At five the hill on which I designed to preach was covered from the top to the bottom. I never saw so large a number of people together, either in Moorfields or at Kennington Common.

Wesley's Journal, 30 May 1742

By the late 1740s, Methodism had grown beyond the original seven circuits to also include Lancashire and Ireland, and Wesley's first visits to East Anglia and Scotland were only a few years away. In ten years it had grown from a few hundred people meeting in Bristol and London, to become a national movement with eighty societies regularly meeting.

Founding a Movement

Key learning points

Ledership Skills

Begin small, grow slow. For three years Wesley constantly travelled between just two centres, resolving disputes and nurturing the fledgling movement. The wisdom learned in organizing these two societies could then be applied on a national scale.

Communicate requirements clearly. The constant rules for societies, bands, classes and preachers clarified expectations for all parties, whilst allowing people to personally fit in and become part of Methodism.

Create a wide team. National evangelists, regional preachers, society leaders, class leaders, band leaders and more were all drawn into involvement. A movement can only grow when it continually includes the involvement of new leaders.

Allow members to use their unique gifts. Whitefield was the greatest preacher of the group; Charles Wesley a gifted evangelist and hymn writer; Wesley a great leader, administrator and discipler.

Treat theological disputes with grace. Seek to minimize conflict and maintain relationships, but refuse to compromise on core issues.

Treat team disunity with discipline. Theological differences can be discussed, but deliberate criticism and back-biting of team members requires prompt action.

Treat violent opposition with courage. 'Always look a mob in the eye.' Win over the leaders of opposition, and you will then win over their followers.

Mission Skills

Be confident in evangelism. Create interest in people, and then expect them to respond.

Develop a structure for discipleship. Methodism's different meetings (field-preaching, society meetings, class meetings, band meetings) encouraged a process of spiritual growth in members.

6

Getting Married

1748–51

Wesley had been without romance in his life since the episode with Sophia Hopkey. But the Methodist Conference of 1748 decreed that it was good for a Methodist preacher to have a wife, so Wesley began to look for a suitable woman. Within three years both John and Charles would be married, but they would have vastly different fortunes.

Grace Murray

Grace Murray was a young widow who ran the Newcastle Orphan House and oversaw the female bands of the local society. In 1748, after four days of her hospitality, Wesley decided she was the woman destined to become his wife.

A Proposal

In August . . . I was taken ill at Newcastle. Grace Murray attended me continually. I observed her more narrowly than ever before, both as to her temper, sense and behaviour. I esteemed and loved her more and more. And, when I was a little recovered, I told her, sliding into it I know not how, 'If ever I marry, I think you will be the person.' After some time I spoke to her more directly. She seemed utterly amazed, and said, 'This is too great a blessing for me; I can't tell how to believe it. This is all I could have wished for under Heaven, if I had dared to wish for it.'

An Account of an Amour of John Wesley[1]

Wesley's half proposal to Grace Murray is reminiscent of the non-committal words he used when talking with Sophia Hopkey ('Miss Sophy, I should think myself happy if I was to spend my life with you'), and his lack of clarity with her – and possibly with himself – is one of the best ways to account for all that subsequently happened in his turbulent relationship with Grace. Perhaps Wesley was deliberately vague because Methodist rules required him to gain the consent of his brother, and the other key leaders within Methodism, before he could marry. He knew this would take time, but he seems to have been in no rush, and did not make his feelings and half-engagement to Grace known to anyone.

After this proposal Wesley took Grace on a preaching tour around Yorkshire, and then left her in the care of one of his most trusted and valued preachers, John Bennet. There was a problem though. Bennet had also recently been nursed through an illness by Grace, and he too had fallen in love with her. Not knowing of her recent engagement to Wesley, Bennet also proposed to her. She initially made no reply, but after two days agreed to an engagement. She would later claim not to have understood Wesley, and not to have believed there was a prior engagement between them. Bennet only became aware of the relationship between Wesley and Grace through a dream.

John Bennet's Dream

John Bennet afterwards told me, that on that very night after he had engaged to Grace Murray, just after he lay down in bed and before he had slept at all, he 'saw her sitting as in deep distress. Mr Wesley came to her with an air of tenderness and said, "I love thee as well as I did on the day when I took thee first." But she put him away from her with her hand.' In the morning, instead of writing to me, he asked her, 'Is there not a contract between you and Mr Wesley?' Partly out of love to him, partly out of fear of exposing me, she replied, 'There is not.'

An Account of an Amour of John Wesley[2]

With Bennet and Grace now engaged, the two wrote to Wesley for permission to marry, as they were required to by Methodist rules. Wesley misunderstood the letters and thought they were already married, so hid his feelings and 'wrote a mild answer to both'.[3] Grace then replied in such an affectionate manner that he realized she was not yet married. They renewed their relationship, and after a winter of confusion for poor Grace, he convinced her that *his* engagement to her was prior to that of Bennet's. In all this he still told no one else of their agreement. She accompanied him on a short tour through Wales in April 1749 (a trip which also included Charles Wesley's wedding to Sally Gwynne) and then on a three month preaching tour around Ireland. According to Wesley, they fell more in love with each other during these months, and just before leaving Ireland for Bristol they allegedly exchanged vows privately in Dublin. This was not quite a marriage, but it was a serious commitment to engagement.

A Love Triangle Crisis

Things began to go wrong again for Wesley when they arrived back in England in July 1749. In Bristol Grace heard rumours of Wesley having a close relationship with another woman, became jealous, and wrote a love letter to Bennet. When they arrived back in Yorkshire Bennet met them, and again pressed his claim. Wesley for a time was unsure what to do, but finally asked Grace to decide between them in early September. In his version of events, 'she declared again and again, "I am determined by conscience, as well as inclination, to live and die with you"' (*An Account of an Amour of John Wesley*).[4]

Having had Grace's final decision, Wesley then wrote to Bennet, setting out his version of all that had happened since his proposal to Grace, and telling Bennet to stop claiming her. He ended the letter: 'Oh that you would take Scripture and reason for your rule instead of blind and impetuous passion! I can say no more, only this, – You may take her away by violence. But my consent I cannot, dare not give: nor, I fear, can God give you His blessing' (letter from John Wesley to John Bennet, 7 September 1749).[5] The letter was to be sent to Bennet by the hand of a man called William Shent. Wesley also made another copy and sent it to his brother. The copy destined for Bennet was never delivered, but Charles, on receiving his copy, learned for the first time that his brother planned to marry.

Charles was furious when he got the letter, and immediately set out from Bristol to Leeds, where he believed his brother and Grace were. He was against the marriage for three reasons: he believed that Grace was little more than a servant, and therefore beneath his brother; he was close friends with Bennet, and knew Bennet to be engaged to Grace; and he was generally afraid that if his brother married anyone, the Methodist movement would suffer from a lack of Wesley's time, and begin to collapse. He rode the length of England, determined to stop the marriage at all costs, travelling from Bristol to Leeds, to Newcastle, and on to the Cumbrian town of Whitehaven, where he finally caught up with Wesley.

Wesley was amazed to see his brother so distressed and against the marriage. He found Charles was too impatient to listen, so he wrote down an account of all that had happened between Grace, himself and Bennet over the previous year. He gave it to Charles, and suggested they allow Vincent Perronet to arbitrate between him and Bennet. Perronet was a vicar in Kent, much respected by them all, and a friend to the Methodist movement. Charles agreed to this, but then deceived his brother. He learned that Grace was currently staying in Allendale, near Newcastle, so galloped off to find her, took her on his horse to Newcastle, and refused to leave until he had seen her married to Bennet. When Wesley himself returned to Allendale, expecting to be reunited with his beloved Grace, he found a quite different set of circumstances. He was left with a choice of whether to chase after Charles and fight for the women he loved in Newcastle, or return to Whitehaven, where he was expected for another series of meetings, and where a mini-revival was taking place. He chose to return to Whitehaven, to preach and to found a Methodist society.

Choosing Ministry Over Marriage

[27 September 1749] Hannah Broadwood, at whose house I left Sister Murray, met me at a little distance from it, and said, 'Mr Charles left us two hours since, and carried Sister Murray behind him.' I said, 'The Lord gave, and the Lord hath taken away: blessed be the name of the Lord!'

[28 September 1749] I need add no more, than that if I had had more regard for her I loved than for the work of God I should now have gone straight on to Newcastle, and not back to Whitehaven. I knew this was giving up all; but I knew God called, and therefore on Friday the 29th I set out again for Whitehaven.

Wesley's Journal

The night before leaving Whitehaven, Wesley had a dream where he saw Grace being sentenced to death, being hung, and then being laid down on a bed, her face having turned black. He took this as a sign that she was no longer his, but had been married to Bennet, so he was prepared for the news when he caught up with Charles and the newly married Mr and Mrs Bennet in Leeds. Fortunately for Methodism, George Whitefield and John

Nelson were also present, and worked hard to reconcile the two brothers.

John and Charles Reconciled

My brother came . . . I felt no anger. Yet I did not desire to see him. But Mr Whitefield constrained me. After a few words had passed, he [Charles] accosted me with, 'I renounce all intercourse with you, but what I would have with an heathen man or a publican.' I felt little emotion. It was only adding a drop of water to a drowning man. Yet I calmly accepted his renunciation, and acquiesced therein. Poor Mr Whitefield and John Nelson burst into tears. They prayed, cried, and entreated, till the storm passed away. We could not speak, but only fell on each other's neck.

John Bennet then came in. Neither of us could speak. But we kissed each other and wept. Soon after, I talked with my brother alone. He seemed utterly amazed. He clearly saw, I was not what he had thought, and now blamed her only.

An Account of an Amour of
John Wesley[6]

Having created such a crisis through his whirlwind of action, Charles finally listened to his brother. He realized that it was not so much Wesley stealing a woman already engaged to Bennet as the other way around. But Wesley had lost the one woman who he ever truly loved, and who might have brought him happiness as a wife, as well as supporting his ministry. His reconciliation with Charles was enough for them to continue working together, and so save Methodism from splintering apart, but they were never as close as they had formerly been. As well as a bride, Wesley also lost one of his best preachers, since just a couple of years later Bennet left Methodism, taking his societies in Bolton and the surrounding area with him. The breach was supposedly over theology, but the facts surrounding Bennet's marriage certainly would not have helped.

The Bennets Leave Methodism

At night I was grieved to hear, in all places, from my coming into Cheshire till now, that John Bennet was still speaking all manner of evil; averring, wherever he came, that Mr Wesley preached nothing but Popery, denying justification by faith, and making nothing of Christ. Lord, lay not this sin to his charge!

Wesley's Journal,
26 March 1752

Molly Vazeille

Within sixteen months of the crisis with Grace Murray, Wesley married someone else. Molly Vazeille was a 41-year-old widow, with independent money and four children. Wesley was 48 when he married her, but seems to have known little about her. Having had Charles ruin his previous engagement, he took no chances this time. Rather than asking permission of his brother and the other senior preachers, as he should have done according to his own rules, he simply informed them of his decision.

Charles's Reaction to Wesley's Engagement

My brother returned from Oxford, sent for and told me he was resolved to marry! I was thunderstruck, and could only answer he had given me the first blow, and his marriage would come like the *coup de grâce*. Trusty Ned Perronet followed, and told me the person was Mrs Vazeille – one of whom I never had the least suspicion. I refused his company to the chapel, and retired to mourn with my faithful Sally. Groaned all the day, and several following ones, under my own and the people's burden. I could eat no pleasant food, nor preach, nor rest either by night or by day.

Charles Wesley's Journal, 2 February 1751[7]

It was a short engagement. On 10 February Wesley slipped on the ice on London Bridge and sprained his ankle. Since he could not travel, and could only preach kneeling down, he decided this would be the ideal time to marry. And so a rift with his brother and a sprained ankle hastened Wesley into a very unhappy marriage. Charles was not invited to the ceremony, and he was not the only one to disapprove of the match: 'At the Foundery I heard my brother's lamentable apology [for marrying Mrs Vazeille], which made us all hide our faces. Several days afterwards I was one of the last that heard of his unhappy marriage' (Charles Wesley's Journal, 17 February 1751).[8]

Wesley took one week off after his wedding to be with Molly and allow his ankle to heal. He then presided over the annual Methodist Conference, and as soon as he could ride again left for a two month preaching trip around the Midlands, Newcastle and Scotland. 'I cannot understand how a Methodist preacher can answer it to God to preach one sermon or travel one day less in a married than in a single state. In this respect surely, "it remaineth, that they who have wives be as though they had none"' (Wesley's Journal, 19 March 1751). Wesley's attitude does much to show why his marriage was not a success. He refused to change his lifestyle to accommodate Molly, and she could not adapt to his itinerant schedule. She accompanied him on some preaching tours in the early 1750s, going as far as experiencing some Methodist persecution through stone-throwing and riots in Hull, but with four children from a previous marriage she could not remain constantly on the road. She therefore began to stay in London while her husband toured the British Isles. However, without him at home she would hear of his pastoral friendships with many women, read some of his letters to female correspondents, and become filled with jealousy. She accused him of having affairs with his housekeepers, and so the London home that Wesley returned to was far from a happy one. By the end of the 1750s the marriage had badly broken down.

Marital Breakdown

Dear Molly – I will tell you simply and plainly the things which I dislike. If you remove them, well. If not, I am but where I was. I dislike (1) Your showing any one my letters and private papers without my leave   . . . I dislike (2) Not having the command of my own house, not being at liberty to invite even my nearest relations so much as to drink a dish of tea without disobliging you. I dislike (3) The being myself a prisoner in my own house; the having my chamber door watched continually so that no person can go in or out but such as have your good leave. I dislike (4) The being but a prisoner at large, even when I go abroad, inasmuch as you are highly disgusted if I do not give you an account of every place I go to and every person with whom I converse. I dislike (5) The not being safe in my own house. My house is not my castle. I cannot call even my study, even my bureau, my own. They are liable to be plundered every day . . . I dislike (6) Your treatment of my servants (though, indeed, they are not properly mine). You do all that in you lies to make their lives a burthen to them. You browbeat, harass, rate them like dogs, make them afraid to speak to me. You treat them with such haughtiness, sternness, sourness, surliness, ill-nature, as never were known in any house of mine for near a dozen years. You forget even good breeding, and use such coarse language as befits none but a fishwife. I dislike (7) Your talking against me behind my back . . . I dislike (8) Your slandering me, laying to my charge things which you know are false . . . I dislike (9) Your common custom of saying things not true . . . I dislike (10) Your extreme, immeasurable bitterness to all who endeavour to defend my character . . . breaking out even into foul, unmannerly language, such as ought not to defile a gentlewoman's lips if she did not believe one word of the Bible.

Letter from John Wesley to Molly Wesley,
23 October 1759[9]

Troubled Marriage

Wesley had shown in his relationship with Grace Murray – when Charles took her to marry John Bennet and Wesley returned to preach in Whitehaven – that his ministry was more important to him than marriage. This continued to be the case when he married Molly. If he had married Grace he might have had a good family life, since Grace was happy to travel with him and be a partner in his work (though she too would no doubt have been jealous and hurt by his close friendships with other women). However, with Molly this was never a serious option. Wesley would intermittently make attempts at reconciliation but, since he was never willing to compromise anything in his lifestyle, they never came to anything.

Wesley the Optimist

I still love you for your indefatigable industry, for your exact frugality, and for your uncommon neatness and cleanliness, both in your person, your clothes, and all things round you. I value you for your patience, skill, and tenderness in assisting the sick. And if you could submit to follow my advice, I could make you an hundred times more useful both to the sick and healthy in every place where God has been pleased to work by my ministry. O Molly, why should these opportunities be lost? . . . If you really are of the same mind with me, if you want to make the best of a few days, to improve the evening of life, let us begin today! And what we do let us do with our might. Yesterday is past, and not to be recalled: tomorrow is not

> ours. Now, Molly, let us set out: 'Let us walk hand in hand to Immanuel's land!'
>
> *Letter from John Wesley to Molly Wesley,*
> *12 July 1760*[10]

Throughout the 1760s Molly and Wesley shared a house together when Wesley was at home in London, but they shared little else, apart from arguments. His independence from her, and lack of care for her, is shown from a journal entry when she became ill: 'Hearing my wife was dangerously ill, I took chaise immediately and reached the Foundery before one in the morning. Finding the fever was turned and the danger over, about two I set out again, and in the afternoon came (not at all tired) to Bristol' (Wesley's Journal, 14 August 1768).

Final Separation

Having temporarily left Wesley several times, Molly finally left for good in 1771: 'For what cause I know not to this day, Molly set out for Newcastle, purposing "never to return". *I did not desert her: I did not send her away: I will not recall her*' (Wesley's Journal, 23 January 1771). They seldom met during the 1770s. One time when they did so, Wesley invited her to come back to him unconditionally, but then regretted it the following day, and asked first for a written acknowledgement that he was innocent of all the affairs she had accused him of.

Unlikely Reconciliation

'All you can do now, if you are ever so willing, is to unsay what you have said. For instance, you have said over and over that I have lived in adultery these twenty years. Do you believe this, or do you not? If you do, how can you think of living with such a monster? If you do not, give it me under your hand. Is not this the least you can do?'

Letter from John Wesley to Molly Wesley,
1 September 1777

Wesley's last contact with Molly was a brief letter he sent in 1778, which concluded with, 'If you were to live a thousand years, you could not undo the mischief that you have done. And till you have done all that you can towards it, I bid you farewell' (letter from John Wesley to Molly Wesley, 2 October 1778).[11] Molly died in 1781, but Wesley was not told of her death for several days, and consequently missed the funeral. From all her possessions, she only left him the wedding ring he had given her thirty years earlier.

Getting Married

Key learning points

Spiritual Formation

Avoid secrecy in relationships. The secrecy surrounding Wesley's engagement to Grace Murray contributed to the confusion, misunderstandings and breakdown of many friendships.

Don't rush into marriage. Choosing a marriage partner is the most important decision in life, and the one that carries with it the greatest responsibility. Marrying an unsuitable partner can devastate many lives.

Marry someone who supports your ministry. Since Wesley's life was so consumed with a vision, it was critical he marry someone who supported that work. Grace Murray could have been that person. Molly Vazeille was not.

Invest time in your marriage. A marriage can only remain strong when both partners commit time to being with each other, listening, serving and loving one another.

Beware of deep friendships with the opposite sex after marriage. Intimate friendships have the potential to become emotionally more than just friendship, and can create jealousy in a marriage partner. Deep emotional relationships can run into sexual relationships – both are forms of betrayal and adultery.

Compromise is necessary. Had Wesley compromised by travelling less, or by writing fewer letters to female friends, his marriage may have survived, and been a source of strength rather than frustration to him.

7

Persevering in Love

1751–71

As Methodism continued to grow, Wesley settled into a routine of travelling, writing, preaching and teaching. He would spend the rest of his life persevering in this work, reconciling preachers and societies, disciplining errant members, and zealously labouring in the movement he had founded.

Severe Illness

Following his marriage, Wesley quickly resumed his busy schedule of work. The only thing that could disrupt his plans for travelling and preaching were either severe bad weather, or serious illness. Bad weather was a constant enemy, although he did have some miraculous stories of God preserving him in the midst of it. When riding through Cumbria in 1753, he recorded: 'A black hail-cloud was driven full upon us by a strong north-east wind, till, being just over us, it parted asunder, and fell on the right and left, leaving us untouched. We observed it the more, because three several storms, one after another, went by in the same manner' (Wesley's Journal, 14 April 1753).

Bad health was a more serious issue, and in November 1753 Wesley found himself severely ill with tuberculosis. He was forced to stop preaching, and being convinced that he was on the verge of death, wrote out an epitaph for his gravestone. However, in the new year his health improved, and he began to preach again in March 1754, although he still did not travel much during the remainder of the year.

Wesley's 1753 Epitaph

Here lieth the body
OF
JOHN WESLEY,
A BRAND PLUCKED OUT OF THE BURNING:
WHO DIED OF CONSUMPTION IN THE FIFTY-FIRST
YEAR OF HIS AGE,
NOT LEAVING, AFTER HIS DEBTS ARE PAID,
TEN POUNDS BEHIND HIM:
PRAYING,
GOD BE MERCIFUL TO ME, AN UNPROFITABLE
SERVANT!

Wesley's Journal, 26 November 1753

Travel Routine

By 1755 Wesley had recovered sufficiently to resume his fixed two-year schedule of visiting and preaching around the British Isles, something that became fairly constant until his death in 1791. He would spend the winter months in London, preaching regularly at the Foundery and other societies across the capital, and still

Wesley's Travel Routine

Year 1

Year 2

proclaiming the gospel to huge crowds of people in the public areas of Moorfields and Kennington Common. When the weather improved in the spring, he would travel to Bristol for a visit of a week or so, before heading north. He would pass through the West Midlands, and up the west coast of England through Lancashire and Cumbria, then into Scotland – spending up to a month or two visiting across the nation – and then travelling back down the east coast of England, spending much time in Newcastle, Yorkshire and Lincolnshire, and coming back to London through the East Midlands. By now it would be late summer, and after hosting the week-long British Methodist Conference (in Leeds, London or Bristol) he would spend another month in Bristol, before returning to London for the winter. However, he would usually take a two week trip to Norwich and East Anglia in November, and another, in December, to the societies across Kent.

After winter in London, he would set out for Ireland in March, sailing there from either north Wales or north-west England. Arriving in Dublin, he would remain a week or so in the city, and then spend four months travelling around the whole of Ireland, usually in a clockwise direction going through Leinster, Munster, Connaught and Ulster. By July he would return to Dublin, host the Irish Methodist Conference, and then sail to England for the British Methodist Conference. The late summer and early autumn months would be spent in Bristol, possibly in visiting south Wales, and in a preaching tour around Devon and Cornwall, before returning to Bristol and ultimately to London for the winter, again with visits to Oxfordshire, East Anglia and Kent before Christmas. In this manner Wesley was able to travel through most of the British Isles over a two-year period, whilst still spending extended time in his English bases of London, Bristol and Newcastle, and to an extent Dublin when in Ireland.

Methodism had now begun to spread further than Wesley's travel schedule. In the 1760s many English people were emigrating to the new colonies of America, and those who were Methodists naturally set up Methodist societies when they arrived in the New World – the first ones were in New York and Maryland. These societies asked Wesley to send more preachers, and the 1769 British conference sent Richard Boardman and Joseph Pilmoor in response – they were the first Methodist missionaries to America. In 1771 Francis Asbury, who would be labelled the 'Wesley of America' and become one of the key leaders in the American Methodist Church, was sent as a missionary to the New World.

Disciplining Society Members

In each place Wesley travelled, he would generally preach at an open-air meeting, at the society meeting, and then spend time visiting some of the classes and bands with the local leaders. He retained his passion for evangelism and for field-preaching throughout his whole life, but he now added an even greater focus on discipleship when visiting the societies. He would often interview the society members to see how they were getting on in their walk with God, and he would remove from membership any who were tolerating sin in their lives. A particular issue at coastal towns was handling smuggled goods, and Wesley spoke severely to the societies in Cornwall, Dover and Sunderland about how this practice was against both the law of England and the law of God.

Smugglers Rebuked

[4 June 1757] In the evening I preached at Sunderland. I then met the society, and told them plain none could stay with us unless he would part with all sin – particularly, robbing the king, selling or buying run goods, which I could no more suffer than robbing on the highway. This I enforced on every member the next day. A few would not promise to refrain, so these I was forced to cut off. About two hundred and fifty were of a better mind.

[23 June 1759] I spoke to each of the society in Sunderland. Most of the robbers, commonly called smugglers, have left us; but more than twice the number of honest people are already come in their place. And if none had come, yet should I not dare to keep those who steal either from the king or subject.

[3 December 1765] I rode to Dover, and found a little company more united together than they have been for many years. Whilst several of them continued to rob the king, we seemed to be ploughing upon sand; but since they have cut off the right hand, the Word of God sinks deep into their hearts.

Wesley's Journal

Wesley was astute enough to realize that a tolerance of sin in just one person could spread through and destroy a whole society. Therefore, he constantly emphasized that members should be accountable and confess sins to each other through the band system, and he acted quickly to dismiss members who did not live up to Methodist rules. A smaller, but holier, society would act as a greater influence for the kingdom on the local town than a large, but indifferent, one. Whilst attendance at field-preaching would usually increase when Wesley visited a town, the membership at the society would actually often decrease, since he would rebuke and expel any who did not live up to the required standards.

A Wesleyan Rebuke

I met the [Norwich] society at seven, and told them in plain terms that they were the most ignorant, self-conceited, self-willed, fickle, untractable, disorderly, disjointed society that I knew in the three kingdoms. And God applied it to their hearts so that many were profited; but I do not find that one was offended.

Wesley's Journal,
9 September 1759

Perfection

This zeal for 'scriptural holiness' in his followers led to one of the most controversial elements in Wesley's preaching – a belief that Christians could reach perfection and freedom from sin in their life on earth. He was aware that this doctrine would be misunderstood by many, and constantly pointed out that perfection did not mean believers would experience freedom from mistakes, from wrong decisions, from illness, or from temptations. He referred to it as 'perfection in love' or as being 'renewed in love', and used it to describe a person who was so consumed with love for God that they no longer sinned in word, deed, thought or feeling.

Perfection Defined

Q. What is Christian Perfection?
A. *The loving God with all our heart, mind, soul and strength. This implies that no wrong temper, none contrary to love remains in the soul; and that all the thoughts, words, and actions are governed by pure love.*
Q. When may a person judge himself to have attained this?
A. *When, after having been fully convinced of inbred sin, by a far deeper and clearer conviction than that which he experienced before justification, and after having experienced a gradual mortification of it, he experiences a total death to sin, and an entire renewal in the love and image of God, so as to 'rejoice evermore,' to 'pray without ceasing,' and 'in every thing to give thanks.' Not that 'to feel all love and no sin,' is a sufficient proof. Several have experienced this for a time, before their souls were fully renewed. None, therefore, ought to believe that the work is done, till there is added the testimony of the Spirit, witnessing his entire sanctification as clearly as his justification.*

A Plain Account of Christian Perfection, 1765[2]

In the early 1760s Wesley instructed his preachers to begin teaching that this perfection was possible on earth, and encouraged them to expect and be on the lookout for it in society members. Perfection was a gift of God, just like salvation was a gift, but it could also be looked for and prayed for, just like salvation. He was delighted when, in the summer of 1762, he met with many members, across Ireland and England, who claimed to have experienced this perfection. He found too that wherever people had received this perfection in love, there was also an increase in the number of people becoming aware of their sins, and finding salvation in Jesus. The message of perfection gave fresh growth to many of the societies.

Perfection Testimonies

[26 July 1762] Upon further examination I found three or four and forty in Dublin who seemed to enjoy the pure love of God. At least forty of these had been set at liberty within four months. . . . The same, if not a larger number, had found remission of sins. Nor was the hand of the Lord shortened yet. . . .

[28 July 1762] There is a glorious work going on at Limerick. Twelve or fourteen have a clear sense of being renewed; several have been justified this week; and on Sunday night, at the meeting of the society, there was such a cry as I scarce ever heard before, such confession of sins, such pleading with the Lord, and such a spirit of prayer, as if the Lord Himself had been visibly present among us.

[2 August 1762] I rode on to Chester. Never was the society in such a state as before. Their jars and contentions were at an end, and I found nothing but peace and love among them. About twelve of them believed they were saved from sin, and their lives did not contradict their profession. Most of the rest were strongly athirst for God, and looking for Him continually.

[4 August 1762] I rode to Liverpool, where also was such a work of God as had never been known there before. We had a surprising congregation in the evening, and, as it seemed, all athirst for God. This, I found, had begun here likewise in the latter end of March, and from that time it had continually increased till a little before I came. Nine were justified in one hour. The next morning I spoke severally with those who believed they were sanctified. They were fifty-one in all – twenty-one men, twenty-one widows or married women, and nine young women or children. . . . I asked Hannah Blakeley, aged eleven, 'What do you want now?' She said, with amazing energy, the tears running down her cheeks, 'Nothing in this world, nothing but more of my Jesus.'

[6 August 1762] I was informed of the flame which had broken out at Bolton . . . 'Glory be to God, He is doing wonders among us! Since you left us there have been seven (if not more) justified, six sanctified, at one meeting. Two of these were, I think, justified and sanctified in less than three days. Oh what a meeting was our last class-meeting! In three minutes, or less, God, quite unexpectedly, convinced an old opposer of the truth and wounded many. I never felt the abiding presence of God so exceedingly powerful before.'

Wesley's Journal

If preaching on perfection, as well as salvation, was good for the spiritual welfare of a society, the lack of this preaching was conversely detrimental. In the autumn of 1762, Wesley travelled to Cornwall, and was disappointed by the state of the societies, but believed he now knew the reason.

Cornish Disappointments

The more I converse with the believers in Cornwall, the more I am convinced that they have sustained great loss for want of hearing the doctrine of Christian Perfection clearly and strongly enforced. I see, wherever this is not done, the believers grow dead and cold. Nor can this be prevented but by keeping up in them an hourly expectation of being perfected in love. I say an hourly expectation; for to expect it at death, or some time hence, is much the same as not expecting it at all.

Wesley's Journal,
15 September 1762

The doctrine of perfection became one of the cornerstones of Wesleyan theology. Wesley preached and believed in it until he died, but he did change one important aspect of it as he grew older. Formerly, he had believed that those who were 'renewed in love' would always remain in that perfection until they died. Latterly, he found that people in that state could still fall from grace, and could lose their perfection, after having it for a season, if they did not continue in their pursuit of God.

One of the great questions of Methodism was therefore whether Wesley himself ever received this perfection. He never spoke on this subject. In fact, after his conversion experience at Aldersgate in 1738, he rarely spoke about his own relationship with God. One of his private letters to his brother Charles revealingly tells us something of his own Christian journey, and the 'dry seasons' he experienced. In the light of this, it is all the more remarkable that he persevered so much in his own spiritual disciplines, and in his powerful ministry.

Wesley's Relationship with God

In one of my last I was saying I do not feel the wrath of God abiding on me; nor can I believe it does. And yet (this is the mystery) I do not love God. I never did. Therefore I never believed in the Christian sense of the word. Therefore I am only an honest heathen, a proselyte of the Temple, one of 'those that fear God.' And yet to be so employed of God! and so hedged in that I can neither get forward nor backward! Surely there never was such an instance before, from the beginning of the world! If I ever have had that faith, it would not be so strange. But I never had . . . I have no direct witness, I do not say that I am a child of God, but of anything invisible or eternal. And yet I dare not preach otherwise than I do, either concerning faith, or love, or justification, or perfection. And yet I find rather an increase than a decrease of zeal for the work of God and every part of it. I am borne along, I know not how, that I can't stand still. I want all the world to come to what I do not know.

Letter from John Wesley to Charles Wesley,
27 June 1766[3]

Strife Amongst Preachers

However, the doctrine of perfection caused Methodism some problems. Like predestination, it was another theological issue over which preachers could disagree, and which would result in some Methodist leaders leaving Wesley and his 'connexion' of churches. Indeed, throughout the 1750s and 1760s the greatest problems that Methodism faced were caused by local leaders renouncing connection with Wesley to become independent, and taking their local congregations with them.

John Bennet did this in Bolton over predestination (though this disagreement was also coloured by his marriage to Grace Murray). However, Wesley was able to keep a small congregation in Bolton, and by 1762 it had grown sufficiently to be a vibrant part of the perfection revival. A greater problem was caused by James Wheatley, a gifted lay preacher from the Midlands who proved very effective as one of Wesley's helpers until he was accused of adultery in 1751. John and Charles Wesley came together to investigate the allegations, found Wheatley guilty of misconduct, and so expelled him from the connexion. Wheatley went to Norwich and founded the Tabernacle, a Calvinistic congregation that gathered several hundred members and constantly preached against the Norwich Methodist Society, until Wheatley once again fell into disgrace in 1758. He handed over the Tabernacle to Wesley, who merged it with the local Methodists in order to foster unity across the town.

The greatest problem Wesley faced from within his own group of preachers was from Thomas Maxfield. Maxfield had been converted under Wesley's ministry, and became one of the first lay preachers. He rose to become the key local leader at the London Foundery, and Wesley thought of him as a 'son in the faith'. Unfortunately, Maxfield misinterpreted the doctrine of perfection in two ways: firstly, by preaching that perfected members could no longer be tempted by sin; and secondly, by confusing salvation with perfection, and preaching that people were not saved unless they were perfected. He also encouraged dreams and visions amongst the congregation that contradicted the words of the Bible. This continued through 1762, with Wesley attempting to rein in his wayward son, but not wanting to discipline him formally, or remove him from his position.

Things became worse at the Foundery when Maxfield's friend George Bell began preaching that Christ would return and the world would end on 28 February 1763. Maxfield allowed Bell to preach, and encouraged the prophecy to be known around London. By the winter of 1762 both Maxfield and Bell then began spreading rumours against Wesley, so much so that on the first day of 1763 Wesley recorded: 'A woman told me, "Sir, I employ several men. Now, if one of my servants will not follow my direction, is it not right for me to discard him at once? Pray, do you apply this to Mr Bell?" I answered: "It is right to discard such a servant; but what would you do if he were your son?"' (Wesley's Journal, 1 January 1763).

Attempts to reason with Maxfield always came to nothing, and clearly Wesley found it difficult to expel from membership this son in whom he had invested so much time and effort. In the end it was Maxfield who severed the relationship with Wesley, taking many of the Foundery congregation with him to form a new society. George Bell left too, but spent the night of 28 February 1763 in prison, arrested by the local magistrates in case he did something to start the end of the world himself.

A False Apocalypse

Preaching in the evening at Spitalfields on 'Prepare to meet thy God,' I largely showed the utter absurdity of the supposition that the world was to end that night. But notwithstanding all I could say, many were afraid to go to bed, and some wandered about in the fields, being persuaded that, if the world did not end, at least London would be swallowed up by an earthquake. I went to bed at my usual time, and was fast asleep about ten o'clock.

Wesley's Journal, 28 February 1763

Three years later Wesley would estimate that the Maxfield-Bell controversy had cost him 600 members in London: 'I wrote a catalogue of the [London] society, now reduced from eight-and-twenty hundred to about two-and-twenty. Such is the fruit of George Bell's enthusiasm and Thomas Maxfield's gratitude!' (Wesley's Journal, 10 February 1766).

With so many good preachers leaving Methodism, but with new societies and circuits constantly being developed, Wesley continually needed to expand his number of lay preachers. Men from all walks of life, who showed gifts of preaching, were enrolled into the ranks, and some women began to preach and lead society meetings too. A new generation of leaders was now joining the movement, the most capable of whom was John Fletcher, a former Swiss mercenary. Fletcher was working as a tutor in Shropshire when he was converted to Methodism in the winter of 1753–54. He was ordained in the Church of England in 1757, and became vicar of Madeley in 1760. He was one of the few clergymen supportive of

Methodism, and was an able writer who defended and expounded Wesley's theology in print.

Reconciling Societies

Wesley seems to have found it easier to reconcile warring societies than warring preachers. His tactics at the Mountmellick society in Ireland, of listening to both parties, and then bringing them together to hear each other and to pray, were used effectively to remove divisions from many other societies around the connexion.

Dispute Resolution Tactics

[1 May 1758] I strove to put an end to the bitter contentions which had wellnigh torn the society [Mountmellick] in pieces. I heard the contending parties face to face, and desired them to speak at large. God gave His blessing therewith; the snare was broken, and they were all cordially reconciled. Only one person was out of all patience, and formally renounced with us all. But within an hour God broke her heart also, and she asked pardon with many tears. So there is reason to hope they will, for the time to come, 'bear one another's burdens.'

[26 June 1767] Finding some of the most earnest persons in the society [Mountmellick] were deeply prejudiced against each other, I desired them to come face to face, and laboured much to remove their prejudice. I used both argument and persuasion; but it was all in vain.

> Perceiving that reasoning profited nothing, we betook
> ourselves to prayer. On a sudden the mighty power of
> God broke in upon them. The angry ones on both sides
> burst into tears and fell on each other's necks. All anger
> and prejudice vanished away, and they were as cordially
> united as ever.
>
> *Wesley's Journal*

A Medical Practitioner

Aside from his constant work with the Methodist societies, Wesley also became involved in the field of medicine. His passion for the poor, and his concern for their
physical welfare, made him critical of doctors who
charged large amounts of money for seemingly simple
cures. In November 1756 he set up a dispensary in
London that gave out free drugs and remedies for any
person who wanted them. He also became very interested in the new cure of electricity, and set up a machine at
the dispensary for 'electrifying' any person who wanted
to try it. He himself regularly underwent the technique,
and claimed to know no one who had been harmed by it,
and many who had been healed from various complaints:
'I should have been glad of a few days' rest, but it could
not be at this busy season. However, being electrified
morning and evening, my lameness mended, though but
slowly' (Wesley's Journal, 26 December 1765).

He also published, again for the sake of the poor, a
Primitive Physick, a book which claimed to provide 'a
plain and easy way of curing most diseases. . . . Who
would not wish to have a physician always in his house,
and one that attends without fee or reward?'[4]

Examples of Wesley's Remedies

A Cold
176. Drink a pint of cold water lying down in bed: Tried
178. Or, to one spoonful of oatmeal, and one spoonful of honey, add a piece of butter, the bigness of a nutmeg; pour on gradually near a pint of boiling water; drink this lying down in bed.

A Cold in the Head
179. Pare very thin the yellow rind of an orange. Roll it up inside out, and thrust a roll into each nostril.

The Ear-Ache
325. Rub the ear hard a quarter of an hour: Tried.
326. Or, be electrified.
328. Or, put in a roasted fig, or onion, as hot as may be: Tried.
329. Or blow the smoke of tobacco strongly into it.

Primitive Physick, 1772[5]

Use of Time

Wesley was able to combine the roles of preacher, leader, prolific writer and amateur physician because of his strict use of time. Ever since his days at Oxford, he had been conscious of how important time was, and he resolved to do nothing which did not contribute to the work of God. Literally, 99 per cent of his time was spent in personal devotion, preaching, studying, administration, writing letters, or talking with individuals about Christ. (He did take the odd moment off, and would occasionally visit Westminster Abbey, or some other eighteenth-century tourist attraction, but would usually be with a friend so they could talk of spiritual matters.) Even his travelling time was put to good use; he would read whilst riding on horseback, and when he became older and used a carriage more, he fitted it out as a study so he could write letters and read. On one occasion, when his wife Molly was travelling with him and was late in being ready to depart after a service, he stood for ten minutes outside the carriage with his watch in hand, counting down the minutes, and then left without her. This cannot have been good for his marriage, but it proved his zeal in strictly spending all of his time on the work of God – he no doubt thought ten minutes was very gracious. For Wesley, nothing was more important than God bringing an awareness of sin, salvation, and perfection in love amongst his people. This was the vision that he constantly set before himself and his followers. This was what he spent all his time on, and this is what brought him the greatest joy in his life.

Revival at Kingswood School

On Wednesday the 20th God broke in upon our boys in a surprising manner. A serious concern has been observable in some of them for some time past; but that night, while they were in their private apartments, the power of God came upon them, even like a mighty, rushing wind, which made them cry aloud for mercy. . . . For my part, I have not often felt the like power. We have no need to exhort them to pray, for that spirit runs through the whole school; so that this house may well be called 'an house of prayer.' While I am writing, the cries of the boys, from their several apartments, are sounding in my ears. . . . There are but few who withstand the work; nor is it likely they should do it long; for the prayers of those that believe in Christ seem to carry all before them. Among the colliers likewise the work of God increases greatly; two of the colliers' boys were justified this week. The number added to the society since the Conference is a hundred and thirty. . . .

This is the day we have wished for so long; the day you have had in view, which has made you go through so much opposition for the good of these poor children.

Account from one of the schoolmasters,
Wesley's Journal, 5 May 1768

Perseverance

When studying Wesley, one of the most inspiring things is to realize his amazing persistence in his work. For fifty-three years he travelled around the British Isles, preaching the same essential message, and calling people to adhere to the same system of Methodist rules and structure. He never tired of preaching to the people, and he never became too impatient with any of his divided – or even disbanded – societies, to wholly give up on them. When societies were arguing, he reconciled them. When they had given up some of his key practices (such as field-preaching, prayer meetings or band meetings) he would call them back to his simple and proven strategies. When societies fell apart, or key leaders left and took societies with them, he would simply begin again the mission of Methodism in that place.

Starting Again

I reached Cardiff. Finding I had all here to begin anew, I set out as at first, by preaching in the Castle Yard on 'Lord, are there few that be saved?' I afterwards met what was once a society, and in the morning spoke severally to a few who were still desirous to join together, and build up, not devour, one another.

Wesley's Journal, 28 September 1753

Never Tiring of the Message

I preached at Bingham, ten miles from Nottingham. I really admired the exquisite stupidity of the people. They gaped and stared while I was speaking of death and judgment, as if they had never heard of such things before.

Wesley's Journal, 30 July 1770

Wesley's attitude to ministry and perseverance is well summed up by his attitude to the school at Kingswood that he had founded for the children of the coal miners back in 1739. He would regularly spend much of his time when visiting Bristol in reorganizing it, and sorting out issues with the staff team. He continued to persevere because he knew the vision of having the school provide a Christian education and background for the boys far outweighed all the problems he encountered. Even after the flame of revival that burst out there had died down, he simply resolved to persevere once again, in order to see God move amongst the children.

Persevering in Love

I spent an hour among our children at Kingswood. . . . What is become of the wonderful work of grace which God wrought in them last September? It is gone! It is lost! It is vanished away! There is scarce any trace of it remaining! Then we must begin again; and in due time we shall reap, if we faint not.

Wesley's Journal, 6 September 1771

By 1770 there were nearly thirty thousand society members of the Methodist movement. His great perseverance was beginning to pay dividends.

Persevering in Love

Key learning points

Spiritual Formation

Continue to spend time with God. Even during the 'dry seasons' of ministry, Wesley continued to seek God through his regime of personal devotions, and God continued to use him powerfully.

Leadership Skills

Keep in touch with the movement. Wesley's constant travel around his 'connexion' enabled him to keep in touch with leaders and members on the ground. His friendships with people held the movement together.

A movement is only as strong as its leadership. Whenever leaders left Methodism, they would take their own networks of followers with them. New leaders joining the movement would bring new networks with them.

Discipline your leaders, including those you have mentored personally. Wesley's failure to effectively confront Thomas Maxfield led to around six hundred people leaving Methodism, and Maxfield still left in the end. Tackle difficult issues quickly, before they grow to become larger.

Listen to both sides in a conflict. Having people listen to each other and pray together is a powerful strategy when trying to reconcile them.

Manage your time wisely. Make the most of every moment; time is our most precious resource. Wesley used his travel time for personal growth, and work.

Persevere in the work God has called you to. A life given to faithfully serving one vision can have a huge impact on the world.

Mission Skills

Discipline members. The clear standards expected of members of Methodist societies ensured they continued to grow in holiness. Expelling members who contravened the rules actually led to increased membership in the long term.

God can free us from sin. By setting the goal of perfection for Methodists, the people sought God all the more. His power and presence in their lives enabled many of them to conquer sin.

Love the people you are serving. The free medicines given out to the poor helped hundreds of people. Their physical as well as their spiritual health was important to Wesley.

8

Leaving a Legacy

1771–91

Methodism grew more in the last twenty years of Wesley's life – in both the British Isles and across North America – than it did in all its thirty years of previous existence. Wesley continued to work right up to the last week of his life, aged 88, and his last years were consumed with the task of ensuring the movement would survive and thrive after his death.

Reminders of Mortality

Several events happened in the early 1770s to help Wesley think about his own mortality. The great George Whitefield died in September 1770, whilst travelling on his seventh preaching tour across America. Although Whitefield had not worked in full connection with Wesley for over thirty years, and the two men disagreed sharply over predestination, they had maintained a warm friendship, and Wesley delivered the funeral sermon at Whitefield's Tabernacle in London.

In January 1771 Molly Wesley left her husband's home in London, ending any further chances of reconciliation between them. In June 1774, when travelling in a horse-drawn coach just outside Newcastle, Wesley was nearly killed. The horses bolted, knocking the driver off the carriage, and nearly taking Wesley and his companions down the side of a steep cliff. All these events would have reminded Wesley of the fragility of life, and the importance of safeguarding the movement he had begun beyond his death.

Remaining Opposition

By this time it was rare for Methodist preachers to be met with the type of violent mobs they had encountered back in the 1740s. Persecution from the Church of England had also lessened. Methodists were still often reviled or ignored by local parish priests, but they were no longer rounded up and taken to the magistrates, or conscripted into the army. The largest obstacle from outside Methodism now came from within the evangelical movement, in the form of the Calvinistic preachers of Lady Huntingdon's Connexion, who were attempting to steal away Methodist members.

Rival Preachers

[3 July 1779] I reached Grimsby, and found a little trial. In this, and many other parts of the Kingdom, those striplings who call themselves Lady Huntingdon's preachers have greatly hindered the work of God. They have neither sense, courage nor grace to go and beat up the devil's quarters in any place where Christ has not been named; but wherever we have entered as by storm, and gathered a few souls, often at the peril of our own lives, they creep in, and, by doubtful disputations, set every one's sword against his brother.

[28 March 1782] Coming to Congleton, I found the Calvinists were just breaking in and striving to make havoc of the flock. Is this brotherly love? Is this doing as we would be done to? No more than robbing on the highway. But it is *decreed*, they cannot help it; so we cannot blame them.

Wesley's Journal

From within Methodism, the main recurring obstacle that Wesley faced was over control of the pulpits. Wesley was a firm believer in an itinerant preaching system, where preachers only stayed in one place for a time, before moving on to a different circuit. In this way he believed both societies and preachers would remain fresh – he feared one preacher would soon run out of sermons if he continued to preach to the same congregation, and so would bore the congregation and kill any spiritual vitality. Many of his preachers began to disagree though, and would insist on staying at a society or circuit long after Wesley had posted them somewhere else. Disputes of this manner happened in Bristol in 1779, in Birstall in 1783, and in Plymouth in 1784. The key issue in Wesley's mind came to be centred on this aspect of control – when he died, who would be the person to choose where different preachers would be posted?

Choosing A Successor

Wesley had previously tried, without success, to name a successor to his leadership. In the early years it was laid down that his brother Charles would take over the responsibility, should anything happen to Wesley. However, by the 1770s Charles had settled down to family life in London. He no longer travelled, his health was not as robust as Wesley's, and he was out of touch – and out of favour – with many of the newer preachers (due to him being insistent on Methodism remaining within the Church of England, and to him often hogging the pulpits in London). Charles was clearly now unsuitable as a successor, so Wesley turned his thoughts towards his Swiss friend, John Fletcher. Fletcher was from the younger generation, and he was ordained, so could continue Methodism's relationship within the Church of England. He was also skilled as a preacher, a writer and a leader, and his life was considered to be so pure and holy that he was universally popular. In 1773 Wesley wrote him one of the most persuasive and didactic letters of his career:

An Invitation to John Fletcher

Dear Sir – What an amazing work has God wrought in these kingdoms in less than forty years! And it not only continues but increases throughout England, Scotland, and Ireland; nay, it has lately spread to New York, Pennsylvania, Virginia, Maryland, and Carolina. But the wise men of the world say, 'When Mr Wesley drops, then all this is at an end!' And so it surely will unless, before

God calls him hence, one is found to stand in his place. For 'the rule of many is not good; let there be one ruler.' I see more and more, unless there be one 'leader', the work can never be carried on. The body of preachers are not united; nor will any part of them submit to the rest: so that either there must be *one* to preside over *all* or the work will indeed come to an end. . . .

But has God provided one so qualified? Who is he? *Thou art the man!* God has given you a measure of loving faith and a single eye to His glory. He has given you some knowledge of men and things, particularly of the whole plan of Methodism. You are blessed with some health, activity and diligence, together with a degree of learning. And to all these He has lately added, by a way none could have foreseen, favour both with the preachers and the whole people.

Come out in the name of God! Come to the help of the Lord against the mighty! Come while I am alive and capable of labour. . . . Come while I am able, God assisting, to build you up in faith, to ripen your gifts, and to introduce you to the people. . . . What possible employment can you have which is *of so great importance?*

But you will naturally say, 'I am not equal to the task; I have neither grace nor gifts for such an employment.' You say true; it is certain you have not. And who has? But do you not know Him who is able to give them? Perhaps not at once, but rather day by day: as each is, so shall your strength be.

'But this implies,' you may say, 'a thousand crosses, such as I feel I am not able to bear.' You are not able to bear them now; and they are not now come. Whenever they do come, will He not send them in due number, weight, and measure? And will they not all be for your profit, that you may be a partaker of His holiness?

Without conferring, therefore, with flesh and blood, come and strengthen the hands, comfort the heart, and share the labour of, your affectionate friend and brother, John Wesley.

Letter from John Wesley to John Fletcher,
15 January 1773[1]

Fletcher responded by promising to assist Charles in the leadership of Methodism should anything happen to Wesley, to happily act as Wesley's personal servant and helper during the latter years of Wesley's life, and to pray to see if God was calling him to inherit Wesley's mantle. But in the short term, he still felt called to his parishioners in Madeley. However, Fletcher's health was fragile. In 1777 he became severely ill, and had to go to his native Switzerland to recover. He eventually returned to England, but remained in poor health, and died in 1785. Rather than being his successor, Wesley ended up preaching his funeral sermon.

With both Charles and Fletcher out of the picture, there was speculation that, after his death, Wesley intended Reverend Dr Thomas Coke to succeed him. Coke was an Anglican vicar who met Wesley in 1776, and was one of his key supporters and leaders. He became known as the Father of Methodist Missions due to his support of missions to America, Europe, Africa and India, and he was twice elected President of the British Methodist Conference following Wesley's death.

However, Wesley did not appoint Coke as his successor. In fact, having decided that no one apart from

Fletcher would have been able to keep the movement together, he did what was perhaps the only thing left open to him – he officially recognized the Methodist Conference as his successor. The 1784 Deed of Declaration created a group within the Conference called the Legal Hundred, and endowed them with all of Wesley's powers upon his death. This ensured that the movement had stability, and would be more likely to hold together. It also ensured that individual preachers would still not be able to remain where they chose. From Wesley's death the Conference would now take all of these decisions.

America

The future of British Methodism was now planned for, but the situation in America was very different. The American movement had already begun to distance itself from Wesley's authority, and the outbreak of war between Britain and America in 1775 only hastened this process. Most of the Methodist missionaries returned to Britain, as did most of the Church of England clergy. Wesley argued long with the Bishop of London (who was responsible within the Anglican Church for the American mission field) to send more ordained ministers to give the sacraments to the American flock, only for the Bishop to respond that there were already three ministers in America – why did they need any more?

Wesley literally took matters into his own hands, and ordained two of his preachers to serve in America: 'Being now clear in my mind, I took a step which I had long weighed in my mind, and appointed Mr Whatcoat and

Mr Vasey to go and serve the desolate sheep in America'
(Wesley's Journal, 1 September 1784). Being ordained
meant that these men could administer the Lord's Supper
and baptize people, but this was a clear breach with
Church of England policy, since only bishops, not priests,
could ordain people. Even more controversially, he also
laid hands on the already ordained Thomas Coke, conse-
crating him as superintendent minister of Methodist
America, and asking Coke to similarly consecrate Francis
Asbury when he arrived on American soil.

American Methodism was now on the path to becoming
an independent church denomination, with Asbury and
Coke as its co-leaders. Its future was assured, but many of
Wesley's friends in Britain were aghast at what he had
done, especially his brother Charles, who had pledged to
live and die within the Church of England, and who used
his hymn writing skills to publish his displeasure.

An Ordination Hymn

Wesley himself and friends betrays,
    By his good sense forsook,
When suddenly his hands he lays
    On the hot head of Coke.

But we alas should spare the weak,
    His weak Co-equals *We*,
Nor blame a hoary Schismatic
    A Saint of Eighty-three!

So easily are Bishops made
    By man's or woman's whim?

Wesley his hands on Coke hath laid,
　But who laid hands on Him?

Hands on himself he laid, and took
　An Apostolic Chair:
And then ordain'd his Creature Coke
　His Successor and Heir.

Charles Wesley, 1784[2]

Whilst Wesley never regretted the decision to ordain Coke and Asbury, he did come to worry about the way they were conducting themselves. Rather than using the title 'Superintendent', the two referred to themselves as bishops, and when they founded a college they named it Cokesbury College, after themselves.

Advice on Humility

But in one point, my dear brother, I am a little afraid both the Doctor and you differ from me. I study to be little: you study to be great. I creep: you strut along. I found a school: you a college! Nay, and call it after your own names! O beware, do not seek to be something! Let me be nothing, and 'Christ be all in all!'

One instance of this, of your greatness, has given me great concern. How can you, how dare you suffer yourself to be called Bishop? I shudder, I start at the very thought! Men may call me a knave or a fool, a scoundrel, and I am content; but they shall never by my consent call me

Bishop! For my sake, for God's sake, for Christ's sake put a full end to this!

Letter from John Wesley to Francis Asbury,
20 September 1788[3]

Relationship with the Church of England

With clear successors named, both at home and in America, the last remaining issue for Wesley was Methodism's relationship with the Church of England. For fifty years he had fought for Methodism to be a renewing movement within the Established Church, and had prevented his preachers from dispensing sacraments, or from holding meetings during church services. Instead, he had constantly encouraged all Methodists to worship in their local parish church each Sunday. But by the 1780s, although he continued to fight for this ideal, he could see that he was losing the battle.

Methodism and Anglicanism

[24 October 1786] I met the classes at Deptford, and was vehemently importuned to order the Sunday service in our room at the same time with that of the Church. It is easy to see that this would be a formal separation from the Church.

[2 January 1787] I went over to Deptford; but it seemed I was in a den of lions. Most of the leading men of the society were mad for separating from the Church. I endeavoured to reason with them, but in vain; they had neither good sense nor even good manners left. At length, after meeting the whole society, I told them, 'If you are resolved, you may have your service in church hours; but remember, from that time you will see my face no more.' This struck deep; and from that hour I have heard no more of separating from the Church!

[6 July 1788] I would fain prevent the members here from leaving the Church; but I cannot do it. As Mr Gibson [the Epworth vicar] is not a pious man, but rather an enemy to piety who frequently preaches against the truth and those that hold and love it, I cannot with all my influence persuade them either to hear him or to attend the sacrament administered by him. If I cannot carry this point even while I live, who then can do it when I die? And the case of Epworth is the case of every church where the minister neither loves nor preaches the gospel. The Methodists will not attend his ministrations. What then is to be done?

Wesley's Journal

Wesley's ordination of preachers for America had, in effect, declared American Methodists to be an independent church, and had opened the door for the same to happen in England. He could no longer stop the momentum he had created. It would not happen in his lifetime, but he realized he could not prevent the inevitable from happening after his death. The matter was discussed at the 1788 Conference, but even there he conceded that Methodists acted outside of Anglican discipline.

1788 Methodist Conference

The sum of a long conversation was 1) that, in a course of fifty years, we had neither premeditatedly nor willingly varied from it [the Anglican Church] in one article either of doctrine or discipline; 2) that we were not yet conscious of varying from it in any point of doctrine; 3) that we have in a course of years, out of necessity, not choice, slowly and warily varied in some points of discipline, by preaching in fields, by extemporary prayer, by employing lay preachers, by forming and regulating societies, and by holding yearly conferences. But we did none of these things till we were convinced we could no longer omit them but at peril of our souls.

Wesley's Journal, 4 August 1788

Passion for Mission

Wesley's goal in making arrangements for after his death was to ensure that Methodism remained as an active missionary movement, and did not solidify into something resembling the stagnant Established Church that he had been forced to circumvent fifty years earlier. This was always his sole consideration. The frustrations with societies he experienced in these last years – with leaders changing some of his methods – were always governed by an overwhelming desire to ensure the movement did not lose its passion for reaching the lost and serving the least.

Wesley's Main Frustrations with Societies

Stopping Field-Preaching
This was always Wesley's number one fear for the societies. If preachers no longer had the heart to get up early enough to preach the gospel message to workers, then how did they expect to continue to grow as a Christian movement?

Stopping Band Meetings
or Class Meetings
Without the fellowship and accountability these meetings provided, individual members could quickly become cold in their relationship with God.

Stopping Church Attendance
Wesley believed that taking Holy Communion regularly was an important means of grace. He also believed in unity within Christianity, and therefore wanted his followers to remain faithful in Anglican church attendance.

One Preacher Staying Too Long
at One Society
This would result in the congregation becoming bored of the sermons, and would therefore reduce their missionary zeal.

Not Preaching Perfection
Without this goal to live towards, members could plateau, or even go backwards, in their spiritual growth.

Leaving Bristol after preaching at five, in the evening I preached at Stroud; where, to my surprise, I found the morning preaching was given up, as also in the neighbouring places. If this be the case while I am alive, what must it be when I am gone? Give this up, and Methodism too will degenerate into a mere sect, only distinguished by some opinions and modes of worship.

Wesley's Journal, 15 March 1784

In fact, Wesley's dedication to mission remained one of the hallmarks of his ministry until the end of his life. He did not lose his passion for souls until his own soul finally departed this earth, writing to one of his preachers: 'Give me one hundred preachers who fear nothing but sin and desire nothing but God, and I care not a straw whether they be clergymen or laymen; such alone will shake the gates of hell and set up the kingdom of heaven on earth' (letter from John Wesley to Alexander Mather, 6 August 1777).[4] His greatest excitement, when writing in his Journal, was still reserved for recounting stories of large-scale conversions and revivals.

Weardale Revival

Last summer the work of God revived [in Weardale], and gradually increased till the end of November. Then God began to make bare his arm in an extraordinary manner. Those who were strangers to God felt, as it were, a sword in their bones, constraining them to roar aloud. Those who knew God were filled with joy unspeakable, and were almost equally loud in praise and thanksgiving. The convictions that seized the unawakened were generally exceedingly deep; so that their cries drowned every other voice, and no other means could be used than the speaking to the distressed, one by one, and encouraging them to lay hold on Christ. And this has not been in vain. Many that were either on their knees, or prostrate on the ground, have suddenly started up, and their very countenance showed that the Comforter was come.

Wesley's Journal, 4 June 1772

In London and in Bristol, Wesley still visited the prisons to preach to those who were about to be executed: 'I preached the condemned criminal's sermon in Newgate. Forty-seven were under sentence of death. . . . The power of the Lord was eminently present, and most of the prisoners were in tears. A few days after, twenty of them died at once, five of whom died in peace' (Wesley's Journal, 26 December, 1784). But his passion for mission also continued to extend to the least, as well as to the lost. Wesley had long felt more at home in the company of the poor than of the rich – an interesting reversal for such a well-educated man, brought up with the strictest of high church principles. His societies continued to give liberally to the poor, and he himself still took the lead in this, so much so that he spent a week tramping through the snow in 1785 to raise money for them.

Serving the Poor

At this season we usually distribute coals and bread among the poor of the society. But I now considered, they wanted clothes, as well as food. So on this and the four following days I walked through the town and begged two hundred pounds in order to clothe them that needed it most. But it was hard work, as most of the streets were filled with melting snow, which often lay ankle deep; so that my feet were steeped in snow water nearly from morning till evening. I held out pretty well till Saturday evening; but I was laid up with a violent flux, which increased every hour till, at six in the morning, Dr Whitehead called upon me.

Wesley's Journal, 4 January 1785

Wesley did the same in January 1787, and raised yet more funds. Having often preached his famous sermon on the use of money, he continued to live out its three principles: 'Make all you can, save all you can, give all you can'. By 'save' Wesley meant economize and so minimize expenditure – he did not mean hoarding money: 'You may as well throw your money into the sea as bury it in the earth. And you may as well bury it in the earth, as in your chest, or in the Bank of England. Not to use, is effectually to throw it away' (Sermon XLIV).[5] Despite the earnings now made from his writings, he continued to live on the £30 per year he had lived on for the past sixty years, giving the rest of his money away to benefit the poor.

His passion for mission remained a burning fire in him until the very end of his life. In 1789, aged 86, he made this remarkable statement: 'I had a day of rest, only preaching morning and evening' (Wesley's Journal, 21 March 1789). Even at so great an age, his days of rest still showed his enduring passion and energy for the work of God.

An Honoured Man

As he grew into old age, Wesley received the acclaim and love of many in mainstream society. He was given the freedom of the Scottish cities of Perth and Arbroath in 1772, and he became friends with famous men such as the aged Samuel Johnson and the young William Wilberforce. In 1783 and 1786 he made month-long summer trips to Holland, where he was treated as a venerable old man. In England he found that 'the tide is now turned; so that I have more invitations to preach in churches than I can accept of' (Wesley's Journal, 19 January 1783). The greatest turnaround came in Falmouth, scene of one of his most infamous riots back in 1748: 'The last time I was here, above forty years ago, I was taken prisoner by an immense mob, gaping and roaring like lions. But how is the tide turned! High and low now lined the street, from one end of the town to the other, out of stark love and kindness, gaping and staring as if the king were going by' (Wesley's Journal, 18 August 1789).

Wesley's Famous Friends

I hate to meet John Wesley; the dog enchants me with his conversation, and then breaks away to go and visit some old woman.

Remark from Samuel Johnson to James Boswell[6]

Mr Wilberforce called upon me, and we had an agreeable and useful conversation. What a blessing is it to Mr Pitt to have such a friend as this!

Wesley's Journal, 24 February 1789

Decline in Health

Wesley remained in good health until almost the last week of his life, and he continued in his non-stop schedule of travelling, writing and preaching. Each year, on his birthday, he became fond of reflecting on his longevity, usually attributing it to his 4 a.m. rising, his 5 a.m. preaching, and his travelling over four thousand miles per year.

Wesley's Good Health

To what cause can I impute this, that I am as I am? First, doubtless, to the power of God, fitting me for the work to which I am called, as long as He pleases to continue me therein; and next, subordinately to this, to the prayers of His children. May we not impute it as inferior means,

1. To my constant exercise and change of air?
2. To my never having lost a night's sleep, sick or well, at land or at sea, since I was born?
3. To my having slept at command so that whenever I feel myself almost worn out I call it and it comes, day or night?
4. To my having constantly, for about sixty years, risen at four in the morning?
5. To my constant preaching at five in the morning, for above fifty years?
6. To my having had so little pain in my life; and so little sorrow, or anxious care?

Wesley's Journal, 28 June 1788

It was only in his final year that infirmity finally began to overtake him, but he rejoiced he was not a huge burden to anybody, and could still remain useful in the Lord's service, even when his body began to give way: 'I am now an old man, decayed from head to foot. My eyes are dim; my right hand shakes much; my mouth is hot and dry every morning; I have a lingering fever almost every day; my motion is weak and slow. However, blessed be God, I do not slack my labour: I can preach and write still' (Wesley's Journal, 1 January 1790).

Last Days

Wesley's last year of travelling was 1790, but he was still able to take in his usual tour around England and Scotland, with visits to Wales and the Isle of Wight, just as the previous year he had made his final four-month journey around Ireland. He spent the winter of 1790–91 in London, with a trip to Kent in December, but his journal ended abruptly on 24 October 1790. From then on his diary continued recording his daily routine until the last week of his life. (He had recommenced keeping a diary in December 1782, meticulously writing down how he spent the hours of the day in much the same way as he did in Oxford as a Holy Club member, over sixty years previously.) The first page of the new diary also listed three rules: spend an hour in devotion morning and evening, pray seriously, deliberately and fervently every hour, and never speak with anger in conversation.

In early 1791 he preached in churches and society meetings across London, but began to feel tired and unwell in the middle of February. He still visited friends in Chelsea, Twickenham, Islington, Leatherhead and Balham over the next few days, but when coming home on 24 February, he became ill with a fever, and drowsy. He wrote his final letter on this day, to William Wilberforce, encouraging the young politician in his fight against the Slave Trade.

Wesley's Last Letter

Dear Sir, – Unless the divine power has raised you up to be as 'Athanasius against the world', I see not how you can go through your glorious enterprise in opposing that execrable villainy, which is the scandal of religion, of England, and of human nature. Unless God has raised you up for this very thing, you will be worn out by the opposition of men and devils. But if God be for you, who can be

against you? Are all of them together stronger than God?
O be not weary of well doing! Go on, in the name of God
and in the power of His might, till even American slavery
(the vilest that ever saw the sun) shall vanish away before
it.

Letter from John Wesley to William Wilberforce,
24 February 1791[7]

He lived for another five days, spending much of it in
bed, sleeping, but he was still able to talk a little with family and close friends who came to visit him. The day
before dying, he surprised those with him by energetic-
ally breaking out in singing two verses of Isaac Watts'
version of Psalm 146:

I'll praise my Maker while I've breath,
And when my voice is lost in death,
    Praise shall employ my nobler powers:
My days of praise shall ne'er be past,
While life, and thought, and being last,
    Or immortality endures.

Happy the man whose hopes rely
On Israel's God; He made the sky,
    And earth, and seas with all their train;
His truth for ever stands secure,
He saves th' oppressed, He feeds the poor,
    And none shall find his promise vain.[8]

During that final day, as he found it more and more difficult
to speak, he twice repeated the phrase: 'The best of all is,
God is with us.' Throughout the next night, he repeatedly

tried to say the psalm he had earlier sung, but could only manage, 'I'll praise – I'll praise – !'

Wesley's Death

On Wednesday morning [2 March 1791] we found the closing scene drew near. Mr Bradford, his faithful friend, prayed with him, and the last word he was heard to articulate was, 'Farewell!' A few minutes before ten, while Miss Sarah Wesley, Mr Horton, Mr Brackenbury, Mr and Mrs Rogers, Dr Whitehead, Mr Broadbent, Mr Whitfield, Mr Bradford, and Elizabeth Ritchie were kneeling around his bed, according to his often expressed desire, without a lingering groan, this man of God gathered up his feet in the presence of his brethren! We felt what is inexpressible; the ineffable sweetness that filled our hearts as our beloved Pastor, Father, and Friend entered his Master's joy, for a few moments blunted the edge of our painful feelings on this truly glorious, melancholy occasion. As our dear aged Father breathed his last, Mr Bradford was inwardly saying, 'Lift up your heads, O ye gates; be lift up, ye everlasting doors, and let this heir of glory enter in.'

Account of Wesley's Last Days, Elizabeth Ritchie,
8 March 1791[9]

At the time of Wesley's death in 1791, there were around seventy-two thousand members of the Methodist Church in Britain and Ireland, and sixty thousand members across the newly independent United States of America.

A further seventy thousand were estimated to have already died in the faith. Across the British Isles there were over four hundred and seventy Methodist societies, spread across 114 circuits, served by 300 full-time itinerants and roughly two thousand lay preachers. Wesley's legacy was to continue through the Methodist Church that he left behind, through later movements such as the Salvation Army and the Pentecostal tradition that would owe so much to him, and through the teaching and example he continues to leave to the world.

Leaving a Legacy

Key learning points

Spiritual Formation

Remain faithful in spiritual discipline. Wesley's diary re-emerging in his last years shows that his zeal for living a holy life continued until his death.

Use money to bless others. 'Make all you can, save [economize] all you can, give all you can.' Giving is the hardest, but the most rewarding, of these principles.

Look after your health. Wesley attributed his long life to getting up early and being constantly active. He was able to achieve so much because he lived for so long in such good health, having looked after his body throughout his life.

Remain humble. In old age Wesley didn't allow flattery to tarnish his integrity. Those who had previously demonized him now began adoring him, but his healthy view of himself, grounded in his relationship with God, enabled him to remain humble.

Discerning Vision

Remain passionate about mission. Nothing could distract Wesley from his focus on reaching the lost and loving the least. His passion, leading to him preaching and collecting money in the snow whilst in his eighties, would have had a profound effect on his followers.

Leadership Skills

Ensure the movement continues after you leave it. Not having others to continue and build on your successes is a form of failure. Planning for others to be able to succeed and achieve even more than you have managed is one of the greatest rewards of leadership.

Mentor other leaders. If Wesley had spent more time investing in a younger generation of leaders, he would have found it easier to name a successor. His invitation to John Fletcher came too late. Mentor others before thinking of your succession. You will equip a generation of leaders – one can succeed you in the work, and the others will still do great things for God.

Endnotes

All extracts from 'Wesley's Journal' or 'Wesley's Diary' are taken from *John Wesley, The Journal of John Wesley*, ed. Nehemiah Curnock (8 vols; London: Epworth Press, 1916).

1. Childhood – 1703–20

[1] Arnold A. Dallimore, *Susanna: The Mother of John and Charles Wesley* (Darlington, Co. Durham: Evangelical Press, 1992).
[2] Dallimore, *Susanna*.
[3] Dallimore, *Susanna*.
[4] Richard P. Heitzenrater, *The Elusive Mr Wesley* (2 vols; Nashville, TN: Abingdon Press, 1984).
[5] John Wesley, *The Journal of John Wesley*, ed. Nehemiah Curnock (8 vols; London: Epworth Press, 1916).
[6] Wesley, *Journal*.
[7] Dallimore, *Susanna*.

2. The Religious Zealot – 1720–35

[1] John Wesley, *The Letters of Rev. John Wesley*, ed. J. Telford (8 vols; London: Epworth Press, 1931).

[2] Wesley, *Letters*.
[3] Frank Baker, *Charles Wesley as Revealed by his Letters* (London: Epworth Press, 1948).
[4] Wesley, *Letters*.
[5] John Wesley, *John Wesley's Forty-Four Sermons* (Peterborough: Epworth Press, 2000).
[6] John Wesley, *A Plain Account of Christian Perfection* (New York, NY: G. Lane and P.P. Sandford, 1844).
[7] Wesley, *Sermons*.
[8] Wesley, *Letters*.
[9] Wesley, *Letters*.
[10] Baker, *Charles Wesley*.

3. The Failed Missionary – 1735–38

All quoted material in this chapter is taken from John Wesley, *The Journal of John Wesley*, ed. Nehemiah Curnock (8 vols; London: Epworth Press, 1916).

4. Finding a Life's Vocation – 1738–39

[1] Luke Tyerman, *The Life and Times of the Rev. John Wesley, Founder of the Methodists* (London: Hodder & Stoughton, 1870).
[2] George Whitefield, *Journal of George Whitefield* (London: The Banner of Truth, 1960).
[3] Thomas Jackson, *The Centenary of Wesleyan Methodism* (Whitefish, MT: Kessinger, 2005).
[4] Wesley, *Letters*.

5. Founding a Movement – 1739–48

[1] John Wesley and John Bennet, *Minutes of Methodist Conferences of 1744–1748* (London: Wesley Historical Society, 1896).

6. Getting Married – 1748–51

[1] John Wesley, 'An Account of an Amour of John Wesley', in Richard P. Heitzenrater, *The Elusive Mr Wesley* (2 vols; Nashville, TN: Abingdon Press, 1984).
[2] Wesley, 'An Account of an Amour'.
[3] Wesley, 'An Account of an Amour'.
[4] Wesley, 'An Account of an Amour'.
[5] Wesley, *Letters*.
[6] Wesley, 'An Account of an Amour'.
[7] Charles Wesley, *The Journal of Charles Wesley* (Ada, MI: Baker Book House, 1980).
[8] Charles Wesley, *Journal*.
[9] Wesley, *Letters*.
[10] Wesley, *Letters*.
[11] Wesley, *Letters*.

7. Persevering in Love – 1751–71

[1] Wesley, *Christian Perfection*.
[2] Wesley, *Christian Perfection*.
[3] Wesley, *Letters*.
[4] John Wesley, *Primitive Physick: An Easy and Natural Method of Curing Most Diseases* (Eugene, OR: Wipf & Stock, 2003).
[5] Wesley, *Primitive Physick*.

8. Leaving a Legacy – 1771–91

[1] Wesley, *Letters*.
[2] Barrie W. Tabraham, *Brother Charles* (Peterborough: Epworth Press, 2003).
[3] Wesley, *Letters*.
[4] Wesley, *Letters*.
[5] Wesley, *Sermons*.
[6] Caleb Thomas Winchester, *The Life of John Wesley* (Charleston, SC: BiblioLife, 2008).
[7] Wesley, *Letters*.
[8] Isaac Watts, *I'll Praise my Maker While I've Breath* (1719).
[9] Heitzenrater, *Elusive Mr Wesley*.

Bibliography

Whilst every effort has been made to locate sources of information, some remain unfound.

Baker, Frank. *Charles Wesley as Revealed by his Letters* (London: Epworth Press, 1948).

Clark, Eliza. *Susanna Wesley* (London: W.H. Allen, 1886).

Dallimore, Arnold A. *Susanna: The Mother of John and Charles Wesley* (Darlington, Co. Durham: Evangelical Press, 1992).

Heitzenrater, Richard P. *The Elusive Mr Wesley* (Nashville: Abingdon Press, 1984).

Hempton, David. *Methodism and Politics in British Society 1750–1850* (London: Hutchinson Education, 1984).

Jackson, Thomas. *The Centenary of Wesleyan Methodism* (Whitefish, MT: Kessinger, 2005).

Jackson, Thomas, ed. T*he Lives of Early Methodist Preachers* (6 vols; London: William Nichols, 1865).

Millar, Edward. *John Wesley: The Hero of the Second Reformation* (London: The National Sunday School Union, 1928).

Pollock, John. *John Wesley* (London: Hodder & Stoughton, 1989).

Stevenson, George John. *Memorials of the Wesley Family* (London: S.W. Partridge and Co, 1876).

Tabraham, Barrie W. *Brother Charles* (Peterborough: Epworth Press, 2003).

Tabraham, Barrie W. *The Making of Methodism* (London: Epworth Press, 1995).

Tomkins, Stephen. *John Wesley: A Biography* (Oxford: Lion Publishing, 2003).

Townsend, W.J., H.B. Workman and George Eayrs, eds. *A New History of Methodism* (Charleston: BiblioLife, 2009).

Tyerman, Luke. *The Life and Times of the Rev. John Wesley, Founder of the Methodists* (London: Hodder & Stoughton, 1870).

Waller, Ralph. *John Wesley: A Personal Portrait* (London: SPCK, 2003).

Watson, Richard. *The Life of the Rev. John Wesley: Founder of the Methodist Societies* (New York, NY: S. Hoyt, 1831).

Wesley, Charles. *The Journal of Charles Wesley* (Ada, MI: Baker Book House, 1980).

Wesley, John. *John Wesley's Forty-Four Sermons* (Peterborough: Epworth Press, 2000).

Wesley, John. *How to Pray: The Best of John Wesley on Prayer* (Uhrichsville, OH: Barbour Publishing, 2007).

Wesley, John. *The Journal of John Wesley*, ed. Nehemiah Curnock (8 vols; London: Epworth Press, 1916).

Wesley, John. *The Journal of John Wesley in Four Volumes* (London: J.M. Dent & Co, 1913).

Wesley, John. *The Letters of Rev. John Wesley*, ed. J. Telford (8 vols; London: Epworth Press, 1931).

Wesley, John, and John Bennet. *Minutes of Methodist Conferences of 1744–1748* (London: Wesley Historical Society, 1896).

Wesley, John. *A Plain Account of Christian Perfection* (New York, NY: G. Lane and P.P. Sandford, 1844).

Wesley, John. *Primitive Physick: An Easy and Natural Method of Curing Most Diseases* (Eugene, OR: Wipf & Stock, 2003).

Whitefield, George. *Journal of George Whitefield* (London: The Banner of Truth, 1960).

Winchester, Caleb Thomas. *The Life of John Wesley* (Charleston, SC: BiblioLife, 2008).

Going Forward on Your Knees

Lessons from the Life of Hudson Taylor

Joanna E. Williamson

For centuries God has used committed men and women to share his love, lead his people and shape his Church. Whether they feature in the Bible or have been serving God in more recent times we can learn so much from the many leaders and servants who have gone before.

Going Forward on Your Knees tells the story of Hudson Taylor's life using many of his own words, drawing us right into his world. He is one of the most inspirational Christians of all time. An early missionary to China, he overcame significant obstacles – poor health, shortage of money and language issues. He went on to found his own mission organization, the China Inland Mission (now OMF International).

978-1-85078-961-1

Wigglesworth

The Complete Story

Julian Wilson

Few individuals have made such an impact on the world for the gospel as the Yorkshire-born plumber turned evangelist Smith Wigglesworth. Although he died in 1947, he is, arguably, more well-known now than when he was alive. He founded no movement, authored no books, had no official disciples, and no doctrine or theological college bears his name, but through his audacious faith and spectacular healing ministry, Wigglesworth fanned the flames of revival in many countries throughout the world. Thousands came to know Jesus Christ as their Saviour, received divine healing and were delivered from demonic oppression and possession as a result of his ministry.

In this biography, Julian Wilson provides one of the most comprehensive accounts of the life of Smith Wigglesworth to date.

978-1-86024-840-5

Sadhu Sundar Singh

The Remarkable Story of an Indian Holy Man

Phyllis Thompson

'It is better to burn quickly and melt many souls than to burn slowly and melt none.'

Sadhu Sundar Singh

Hours before he intended to kill himself, the young Sundar had a vision of Jesus. Immediately the emptiness that filled his heart was lifted. Despite opposition at home, he soon knew that he had to share his faith throughout India and Tibet. What better way than to put on the robes of a sadhu and to take to the road with no guarantee of food but with a passionate desire to live as Christ did?

978-1-85078-099-1

Through Gates of Splendour

The Five Missionary Martyrs of Ecuador

Elisabeth Elliot

In 1956 the world was stunned by a shocking event . . .

'Mary was standing with her head against the radio, her eyes closed. After a while she spoke "They found one body . . ."'

Missionary history will never let us forget the five young American men savagely martyred by Auca Indians in the jungles of Ecuador as they attempted to reach them with the word of God.

Elisabeth Elliot, widow of one of these men, records the story of their courage and devotion to Christ in the face of danger and difficulty.

978-1-85078-034-2

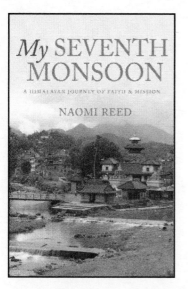

My Seventh Monsoon

A Himalayan Journey of Faith & Mission

Naomi Reed

'The seventh monsoon was the hardest of them all. I sat on the back porch of our Himalayan home and stared as the rain streamed down all around me. I had never felt so hemmed in – by the constant rain, by the effects of the civil war and by the demands of home-school. As I sat there and listened to the pounding on our tin roof, I wondered whether I would make it through. I wondered whether I would cope with another 120 days of rain. And in doing so, I began to long for another season . . .'

From the view point of her seventh monsoon, Naomi Reed takes time to look back on the seasons of her life. As she does so, she shares with us her journey of faith and mission and reveals poignant truths about God and the way he works his purposes in our lives through seasons.

978-1-86024-828-3

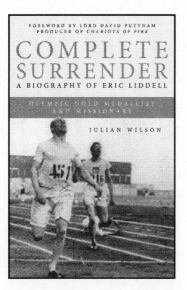

Coming January 2012

Complete Surrender

A Biography of Eric Liddell Olympic Gold Medallist and Missionary

Julian Wilson

'On a stiflingly hot Parisian afternoon in July 1924, six athletes lined up for the start of the Olympic 400 metres. In the sixth and outside lane was the Scottish sprint sensation Eric Liddell . . .'

Liddell made headlines by refusing to race on a Sunday. His switch from 100 metres to 400 metres, and subsequent triumph, is now legendary.

Liddell brought the same singleness of purpose to his faith as to his running. This vivid biography recounts his career as a missionary in war-torn china, his unassuming and selfless character, and his delight in practical jokes. It includes interviews with his family and friends, extracts from his letters and a number of rare photographs.

978-1-86024-841-2